Oliver Hazard Perry
and the
Battle of Lake Erie

Gerard T. Altoff

Put-in-Bay, Ohio

10 October 2000

Oliver Hazard Perry

Oliver Hazard Perry
and the
Battle of Lake Erie

By Gerard T. Altoff

Illustrated by Robyn Opthoff Lilek

THE PERRY GROUP
Put-in-Bay, Ohio

For Those Who Were There

and

In Memory Of
Harold Heidenreich

ACKNOWLEDGEMENTS

A number of individuals provided technical support and assistance, while others reviewed this manuscript to help point out the errors of my way. For their time and effort I would like to thank Cyndee Altoff, Kristin Altoff, Don Cartwright, Phyllis Ewing, Bob Garcia, Sue Judis, Mike Kane, Walter Rybka, Matt Switlik, Laura Thorsen, and Dr. George Vourloujianis.

I wish to express my gratitude to Dr. Peter Rindlisbacher, a great artist, good friend, and truly nice guy—even if he is Canadian—who has been altogether too generous and altruistic in granting me the use of his paintings, past and present. Special thanks go to Robyn Opthoff Lilek, another good friend (you too Mike) whose ability to cheerfully tolerate my constant nagging and harassment is truly amazing, and whose talented drawings grace the pages of this book and my other works.

While mentioned above, I wish to convey additional thanks and appreciation to kindred spirit Phyllis Ewing, superintendent of Perry's Victory & International Peace Memorial. Phyllis's support, encouragement, and friendship have been instrumental in helping complete this project.

Everlasting gratitude, appreciation, and apologies go to my wife, Cyndee, who is probably still wondering if I actually did spend all those nights and weekends in front of the computer.

Finally, publication of this book would not have been possible without the support and sponsorship of The Perry Group, and I wish to relay my heartfelt thanks to The Perry Group board and members.

PREFACE TO REVISED EDITION

The story of the Battle of Lake Erie has often been rehashed. However, most works delve into excessive detail concerning the vessels, fleet movements, principal characters, or the controversies resulting from the involvement of those characters. Obviously these elements are an integral part of the story and are, to a degree, herein related, but often forgotten or ignored in this mass of detail are the stories of the common sailors, soldiers, and Marines who actually fought the battle: who they were, where they came from, what they accomplished, and the sufferings they endured before, during, and after the engagement. Rarely has such a heterogeneous group of men serving on a hybrid fleet combined their efforts for such significant results. Also seldom considered by historians on the southern shores of the Great Lakes and the St. Lawrence River is the plight of the British and Canadian sailors and soldiers; the adversities they faced and the disadvantages under which they fought. The ordeal of these brave men—American, Canadian, and British—is the focus of this book

Since this work attempts to stare into the face of combat, readers should be advised that sections contain vivid descriptions of naval warfare in general, the Battle of Lake Erie specifically, and the resultant wounds suffered by the participants in that engagement. The purpose of relating such detail is not the product of a perverse desire to impart gratuitous violence, nor is it intended as an anti-war statement, although there can be little better method of advocating the benefits of peace than by emphasizing the horrors of war—and the subject of this book is WAR.

Those with first-hand experience know that war is not a kaleidoscope of banners flying, bands playing, long lines of soldiers marching and singing on parade, or politicians spouting jingoistic, meaningless inanities. Once the boredom has been accounted for, war is a tragic blend of mud and blood and hardship and pain and exhaustion and sorrow and misery and killing. Robert E. Lee recognized how easily that war casts its spell. While viewing the awesome and awful spectacle of Union regiments dramatically arrayed in line of battle as they marched in parade ground splendor towards Marye's heights, Lee was heard to mutter, "It is well that war is so terrible—we should grow too fond of it." The ensuing slaughter at Fredericksburg, Virginia on 13 December 1862 bore terrible witness to Lee's insight.

In programs that I offer about military history I have been criticized occasionally for being overly graphic in my portrayal of battle. It is a failing to which I readily admit, especially since those programs are often presented to school groups. I see no reason whatsoever to put a silver lining on the subject of war because if there is one thing I do not wish to do, it is to leave any school child with the impression that there is such a thing in war as glory. Glory is a word that might be intoned by veterans while hoisting a few and toasting fondly remembered comrades at reunions years later, but there is certainly no glory found amidst the pain and anguish in veterans hospitals, and little glory is evident in those vast, sorrowfully symmetrical rows of stark white crosses in veterans cemeteries.

The Battle of Lake Erie was fought in a different era, a time when the term glory was bandied about freely and sought after greedily. For commanders like Oliver Hazard Perry, James Lawrence, Stephen Decatur, David Porter, and Winfield Scott, the quest for glory was desperately and eagerly pursued. The veneer of glory paved the road to promotion and served as a hallmark of peer recognition, a conspicuous badge of professional accomplishment. Men such as these reveled in combat, and the desire for victory was as much for the purpose of self-gratification and personal advancement as it was to achieve the political and military goals of the country. All too often they failed to appreciate that their path to glory was littered with the corpses of men such as Christopher Mayhew, William Cranston, Ethelred Sykes, and Charles Pohig. Thousands did not survive to share in the adulation of the glory hounds, and the families of those men cared not a whit for the glory of war.

This purpose of this book is to tell the story of patriots like David Christie, Joshua Trapnell, William Johnson, George Schofield, and John Silhammer; sailors and soldiers who felt the terror of battle, died horrible deaths, suffered agonizing wounds, or lived with excruciating pain and nightmarish memories for the remainder of their lives. In many cases those lives were drastically shortened as a result of their gruesome wounds and horrific experiences. The reason that their plight is described in such graphic detail is to imprint upon the reader's mind the extent and degree of their selflessness, and to make certain that their sacrifice, and what that sacrifice accomplished, is not forgotten.

Gerard T. Altoff
Put-in-Bay, Ohio

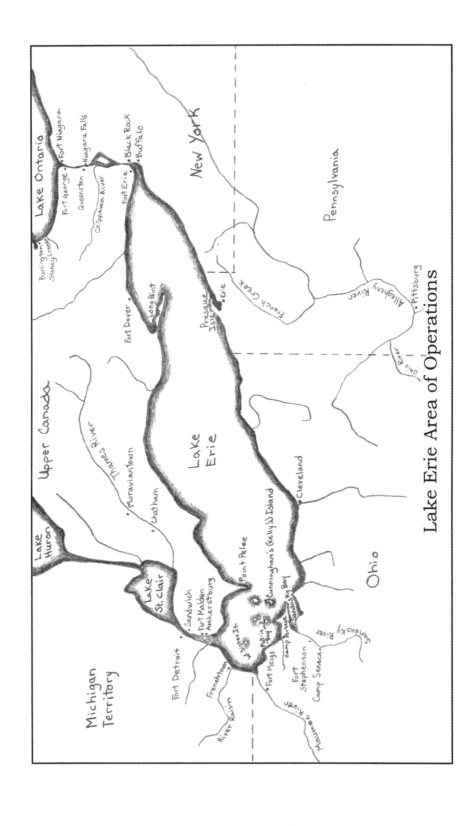

Lake Erie Area of Operations

Oliver Hazard Perry
and the
Battle of Lake Erie

"Our first object is to get a Command of the lakes...This fact assumed, there can no longer be a doubt by what means...the Army assigned to you, ought to approach [the British base at Fort] Malden."[1] So wrote Secretary of War John Armstrong to General William Henry Harrison on 4 April 1813, making it evident to Harrison what his course of action should be for the upcoming invasion of Canada.

Harrison clearly did not need Armstrong's letter to point out what was patently obvious to anyone peering at a map of the western Lake Erie region that fateful spring of 1813. The complete lack of adequate roads, the logistical impediment of the notorious Black Swamp of northwest Ohio,* necessarily attenuated supply lines, and the ability of Britain's Indian allies to interdict any movement of troops and supplies along the western shore of Lake Erie made it readily apparent that a successful campaign against Fort Malden and the Amherstburg Navy Yard, at the mouth of the Detroit River, was dependent upon naval control of Lake Erie.

Lake Erie's strategic importance rendered it a vital link in America's plans to successfully prosecute the war. When the United States declared war on Great Britain on 18 June 1812, a determination had already been made relative to the country's overall goals and objectives; in fact, the methodology on how those goals and objectives were to be achieved had also been decided. America's grievances against the British must be redressed, or so the political dogma of the moment decreed, but the U.S. was not foolish enough to directly attack the fortress-like British Isles, particularly since the U.S. possessed neither an army nor a navy large enough to attempt such a venture. However, north of the U.S. border lay Canada, the nearest British territory, and the U.S. had been casting covetous glances in that direction since the American Revolution—Continental forces unsuccessfully invaded Canada during that conflict.

Canada seemed the logical choice for U.S. attention. In 1812 Great Britain was immersed in a cataclysmic struggle against Napoleonic Europe. Because of Britain's European commitment only a limited number of troops could be spared to fight in North America, a significant factor that

---

* The Black Swamp was a marshy morass blanketing a huge tract of northwest Ohio, with the heart of the swamp lying between the Sandusky River area and the Maumee River. In *Lake Erie*, Harlan Hatcher wrote that the swamp extended southward nearly 100 miles from the lake in some areas. In 1812 the Black Swamp was nearly impassable, and no roads traversed the vast marsh until 1827.

1

influenced many of the political and military decisions rendered by the United States during the years preceding the declaration of war. In addition to few British troops being stationed in Canada, the U.S. population outnumbered that of Canada by more than 10-to-1, and the militant politicians in Congress—those southern and western Democrats commonly referred to as the "war hawks"—shared the erroneous belief that most Canadians secretly wished to be annexed by the United States. Thus America's dominant leadership, prompted by false confidence, concluded that England's colony to the north would prove easy pickings. The battle cry that echoed through the halls of Congress was "On to Canada."

Even before war was declared, the U.S. had developed plans for three separate invasions of Canada; two of those incursions would serve to secure control of Lake Erie. The first offensive occurred along western Lake Erie. In early June of 1812 General William Hull marched north from Dayton, Ohio with an army of 2,500 men. One month later, after a difficult trek through the Ohio wilderness, Hull's army reached Fort Detroit, Michigan Territory. Hull's objectives were Great Britain's principal military installations west of the Niagara frontier: Fort Malden and the Amherstburg Navy Yard, near the mouth of the Detroit River. American forces heavily outnumbered the British, Canadians, and Indians at Fort Malden, but on 16 August 1812, through inept leadership and a series of incredible blunders, General Hull surrendered Fort Detroit and the entire American army virtually without firing a shot.

American fortunes experienced a second embarrassing catastrophe less than two months later. On 12 October a combined force of U.S. regulars and New York militiamen* began crossing the Niagara River opposite Queenston Heights (about five miles north of Niagara Falls). When enemy resistance was encountered by the detachment of regulars, who had embarked first, the New Yorkers waiting on the east bank suddenly developed constitutional scruples and refused to row across the river to help their embattled countrymen. As a result, nearly 1,000 outnumbered American regulars, abandoned by the militia, were either killed or captured.

---

* Regulars were members of the country's standing army, supposedly professional soldiers, but often they were poorly trained and equipped, especially early in the war. Militiamen were citizen soldiers similar to minutemen from the Revolutionary War. After the Revolution the government feared a large standing army, which raised the specter of a military coup, so the militia system was established in order to have a large pool of soldiers available in case of war. Every white male in the U.S. between the ages of 18 and 45 was obliged to serve in a militia unit, and these units were supposed to meet once a month to drill, but monthly musters were largely social occasions. Most militia outfits were poorly armed, poorly trained, and poorly disciplined, and overall they were an ineffective fighting force.

The Battle of Lake Erie

The third offensive, which was to cross the St. Lawrence River and capture Montreal, rapidly degenerated into a farce. In mid-November a 5,000-man army commanded by General Henry Dearborn, half regulars and half New York and Vermont militiamen, gathered just below the Canadian border at the north end of Lake Champlain. When most of the militiamen refused to cross into Canada, Dearborn called his senior officers together for a council-of-war. A consensus was reached to call off the invasion, so Dearborn decided go into winter quarters. Refusing to give up quite so easily was Brigadier General Zebulon Pike. The plucky Pike requested permission to cross the border and, receiving it, assembled a force of volunteers. With about 600 regulars and 400 militiamen, Pike moved against a small British fortification at La Colle Mill (present-day Lacolle, Quebec). Confusion reigned; the British had abandoned the blockhouse and somehow the American militia ended up firing into the U.S. regulars. The error was eventually discovered, but not until the Americans had battled each other for a time and inflicted a number of friendly casualties. In frustration, Pike withdrew back across the border. In less than four months, three major attempts to invade Canada had ended in total disaster.

During the first month of the new year the United States proceeded with another foray against Fort Malden, with distressingly similar results. On 22 January 1813 a small American army of 934 men, led by General James Winchester, was overwhelmed by British and Indians at the River Raisin (present-day Monroe, Michigan). Of Winchester's entire command, only 33 men managed to escape, the remaining 901 were either killed or captured. It was also at the River Raisin where Potawatomi tribesmen massacred approximately 65 American prisoners-of-war, an incident that would be remembered and avenged by fellow Kentuckians less than nine months later.

U.S. forces had squandered several golden opportunities during the first seven months of the war; the British would now assume the offensive. In late April, British General Henry Procter led an expedition up the Maumee River against Fort Meigs, the advanced American supply base erected by Harrison at the rapids of the Maumee (present-day Perrysburg, Ohio). The British surrounded Fort Meigs and opened fire with several batteries of artillery. For two long weeks the British pounded the beleaguered American outpost, and during that period one pitched battle was fought when 1,200 American soldiers sallied against the British artillery; of the attacking force, more than half were killed, wounded, or captured. Even so, the British were unable to breach the fort's stoutly picketed walls and they eventually raised the siege and sailed back to Amherstburg.

Oliver Hazard Perry and

In late July the British invaded the Ohio frontier a second time. Again they sailed up the Maumee River and laid siege to Fort Meigs, and again they were unsuccessful. This time, however, instead of a precipitate withdrawal to Amherstburg, General Procter chose to re-direct his offensive against what he assumed would be a softer target: Fort Stephenson, located about 15 miles up the Sandusky River (present-day Fremont, Ohio). On the afternoon of 2 August 1813, after a one-day bombardment with his artillery, Procter hurled approximately 400 regulars from the 41st Regiment of Foot in a frontal assault against the American stockade. British courage was no match for concentrated American firepower; the redcoats were bloodily repulsed. Procter thereafter loaded his troops and guns back on board his ships and retreated across the lake to Fort Malden.

By the late summer of 1813 America's attempts to invade Canada, particularly along western Lake Erie, had failed miserably. Subsequent British efforts to invade the United States also proved futile. It was now manifest that, for the U.S. at least, one driving factor would determine the outcome of the war in the Old Northwest: control of Lake Erie.

At the outbreak of the War of 1812, Canada's Provincial Marine maintained one 17-gun ship, the *Queen Charlotte*, and several smaller gunboats on Lake Erie. Conversely, the United States had but a single warship on the lake, the brig *Adams*, and this little vessel fell into British hands when General Hull surrendered Detroit. America's entire naval force on Lake Erie, what there was of it, had been easily and completely eliminated shortly after the beginning of hostilities. By mid-August of 1812, British forces were indisputably in control of the lake. In order for the United States to seize the all-important naval advantage on Lake Erie, it would be necessary to start from scratch.

The story of the United States Lake Erie squadron begins with a rather inauspicious incident. On 17 July 1812 the British captured Fort Michili-mackinac—located on Mackinaw Island in the strait between Lake Huron and Lake Michigan—along with its garrison. One of the American prisoners was a man who found himself at the wrong place at the wrong time: Daniel Dobbins. A resident of Erie, Pennsylvania and master of the small merchant schooner *Salina*, the 37-year-old Dobbins and his vessel, by chance anchored at Mackinaw Island, were both included in the surrender terms. Having only a tiny force, the British did not have the wherewithal to cope with all of the prisoners captured at Fort Michili-mackinac. An easy solution for the English commander's problem was to

4

The Battle of Lake Erie

designate the *Salina* and another small schooner, the *Mary*, as cartel* ships. Dobbins and 88 other American prisoners soon set sail for Detroit.[2]

Arriving at Detroit, Dobbins irrationally allowed himself to become embroiled in Hull's ill-fated campaign. He unwisely volunteered to serve with a local militia unit that engaged in skirmishes against the British and Indians, an action that violated his parole from Michilimackinac. When Hull capitulated, Dobbins was transported to Fort Malden with the other American prisoners. There he was recognized as a parole violator and a complaint was filed. Dobbins insisted he never agreed to the parole, but regardless of whether or not he pledged his oath, the undiscerning merchant captain was sentenced to death for his actions. Rather than contest the verdict, Dobbins contrived to make his escape, causing the British to offer a reward for his recapture, dead or alive. A band of Indians set out after the fugitive mariner for both his scalp and the payment, but Dobbins eluded his pursuers and, with some assistance, made his way to Erie. At Erie, General David Mead, commanding the 16th Division of Pennsylvania Militia, ushered Dobbins on his way to Washington, D.C.[3]

Dobbins reached the capital and related his story to Secretary of War William Eustis. The importance of his news eventually gained Dobbins an audience with President James Madison, who, upon hearing details of the Detroit fiasco, called a cabinet meeting to consider the options. Madison and his advisors readily grasped the strategic significance of the country's inland water-borne transportation routes. The Great Lakes and the St. Lawrence River offered ready-made avenues of invasion for whichever nation controlled them, and American leaders realized that one of the country's first priorities should be control of the waterways. For Lake Erie, this would involve building a brand new squadron of warships. Requiring a man to organize and begin the new construction project, and seemingly impressed with what he observed in Dobbins, Madison appointed the merchant captain a warrant officer in the United States Navy. The Navy Department provided Dobbins with a blueprint of a 40-ton gunboat and ordered him to contract for the building of four such vessels. To accomplish this daunting task, Sailing Master Daniel Dobbins was authorized a sum not to exceed $2,000.[4]

Dobbins' first problem was selecting a suitable location to build the gunboats. Naturally he preferred a site familiar to him, so he recommended Presque Isle Bay, conveniently situated at his hometown of Erie, Pennsyl-

---

* A cartel is a written agreement between belligerents for the exchange of prisoners. In this instance the captured Americans were released under the condition that they not take up arms again until properly exchanged.

vania. Presque Isle Bay was an excellent harbor protected on three sides: by Presque Isle peninsula, which jutted prominently into the lake to the north and west, and by the Pennsylvania mainland to the south. But Presque Isle Bay's most conspicuous and favorable feature was its restricted entrance, which permitted access to vessels only via a narrow, winding, and shallow channel cut into the bay's east side. This constricted chute, easily protected with fortifications, would discourage any British naval operation designed to disrupt the ongoing construction project. The Navy Department concurred with Dobbins' selection and ordered him to proceed to Erie without delay.

Dobbins' shipbuilding assignment was not to be an independent one. Recently appointed to the overall command of Great Lakes naval operations was Captain Isaac Chauncey. Commodore* Chauncey had established his headquarters at Sackets Harbor, New York, on Lake Ontario's eastern shore, and Dobbins was ordered to coordinate and cooperate with his new superior. But Dobbins' first attempt to communicate with Chauncey was intercepted by Lieutenant Jesse Duncan Elliott at the Black Rock Naval Station (then just north of Buffalo, New York); Elliott was at that time the U.S. Navy's senior officer on Lake Erie. Without consulting higher authority, Elliott informed Dobbins that Presque Isle was unsuitable for ship construction. Besides, Elliott had recently procured a number of small Lake Erie merchant vessels and had already begun the process of converting them to gunboats at Black Rock. Furthermore, Elliott had contracted for the purchase of materials to begin construction of even larger gunboats at the Black Rock Naval Station. If warships were to be built on Lake Erie, then Black Rock was the logical location, and the current commander of that naval station was the obvious choice to direct such a venture—or so Elliott felt.[5]

Chauncey concurred with Elliott's opinion, particularly in light of the fact that the commodore himself intended to expand the role of Black Rock. Plans to build two 400-ton vessels and three gunboats at the small navy yard were currently being formulated. Those plans changed in late October when Chauncey finally received a copy of Dobbins' instructions from the Navy Department to build four gunboats at Erie. Still uncertain if Erie was the appropriate location for boat building, the commodore reluctantly authorized Dobbins to begin preparations for assembling two 60-ton schooners. Chauncey further advised Dobbins that he would visit Erie himself in the near future. Despite his haggling with Chauncey and

---

* Chauncey's actual rank was that of captain, but since he commanded more than one vessel, in this case the entire Lake Ontario squadron, he was entitled to the honorific of commodore.

The Battle of Lake Erie

Elliott, Dobbins, acting in good faith and spurred by his Navy Department orders, had begun construction at Erie almost a month earlier.[6]

Hired to assist Dobbins with design and production was Ebenezer Crosby, a master shipwright from Niagara County, New York. Chauncey had only authorized the building of two gunboats, but together these two men commenced erecting four vessels, each having 50-foot keels. His original mandate from the Navy Department directed that four gunboats be built, but concerned about possible criticism from his superior, Dobbins complained to Secretary of the Navy Paul Hamilton that no instructions had been received from Chauncey; whether or not Dobbins actually received Chauncey's authorization letter is unknown.[7]

By the time that Chauncey finally visited Erie on 31 December 1812, two of Dobbins' gunboats were on the stocks being framed and the other two were being prepared for framing. The commodore was more than a little disturbed when he viewed Dobbins' progress at Erie. Despite the previous communication from Washington, he had ordered the Erie sailing master to build two gunboats, only to discover that Dobbins had twice that number on the stocks. Chauncey was also displeased by the size of the vessels, feeling that they were too small to be effective against the British. In his own defense, Dobbins denied ever receiving specific directions from Chauncey about how many gunboats to build, and, as for size, he was using the plans supplied to him by the Navy Department. At this point it really mattered little as there was only so much the commodore could do to change the situation. Modifying the two gunboats whose frames were already in place was impossible, but Chauncey did order the other two vessels to be altered, extending them by 10 feet. Chauncey also instructed Dobbins to contract for a larger brig of war, an order that was subsequently expanded to include two brigs of 20 guns each.[8]

It must be said of Chauncey that once he noted the extent of the construction at Erie, despite his earlier reservations, he firmly supported the project. From this point onward the commodore contributed or otherwise secured all available resources, doing everything within his power to procure the supplies and materials needed to fit out the Lake Erie flotilla. Among those resources was Noah Brown, a renowned New York City ship designer and builder. Chauncey communicated with Brown and directed him to "proceed with all possible despatch [sic]for Erie...there to build in the shortest time possible 2 Brigs capable of mounting 18-32 pounders [sic] carronades & 2 long 9's."[9] Chauncey further instructed Brown to take charge of the four gunboats and finish them as soon as possible. Another asset arranged by Chauncey was the services of Sailmaker James Sackett,

Oliver Hazard Perry and

Isaac Chauncey

Daniel Dobbins

also from New York City. The commodore requested that Sackett travel to Erie and "take with you a sufficient number of workmen to enable you to make a Suit of Sails for 2 Brigs and 4 Schooners."[10] At a later date Chauncey also sent a gang of riggers from Sackets Harbor to assist with fitting the Erie vessels.[11]

Following a brief, one-day tour of the Erie construction project, Chauncey departed for the return journey to his base at Sackets Harbor. He anticipated that the vessels would be completed sometime in June, which meant that it was time to devote some thought to assigning a more senior naval officer to finalize construction and fit out the new fleet. The only problem was that Chauncey lacked experienced officers on the lakes and he felt that those among his present complement were deficient in seniority. This dilemma was on Chauncey's mind when he arrived at Sackets Harbor on 19 January 1813, so he was both surprised and pleased by the discovery of a letter that awaited his return. Chauncey needed a commander for the Lake Erie squadron, and 27-year-old Master Commandant* Oliver Hazard Perry was yearning for just such an opportunity.

The man who was to lead the Lake Erie fleet to victory during the War of 1812 was born on 23 August 1785 at South Kingstown, a hamlet near the village of Wakefield, Rhode Island. The eldest of five sons and three daughters born to Christopher Raymond and Sarah Wallace Alexander Perry, the first son was named after his paternal grandmother's father, Oliver Hazard, and also for his uncle, Oliver Hazard Perry, who had been lost at sea a few years before Perry was born. Perry's Scots-Irish ancestry can be traced to the family of William Wallace, the famous Scotsman who led a rebellion against England's Edward I during the late 13th and early 14th centuries.

Barely into his teens, the strong-willed and quick-tempered youth decided to follow the sea. Prior to the establishment of the naval academy a young officer aspirant was required to obtain a midshipman's warrant from the Secretary of the Navy. Acquiring one of the much sought-after appointments proved to be considerably easier if the candidate possessed some type of influence, and the 13-year-old youngster certainly had the necessary connection. During the early months of 1799 the U.S. Frigate *General Greene* was in the process of fitting out for service against France

---

* Master commandant was a rank unique to the United States Navy. In the naval hierarchy it was between lieutenant and captain, and equivalent to a commander in the British Navy. Master commandant was Perry's official rank, but as the commanding officer of a vessel, the *Lawrence*, he was entitled to be referred to as captain, and as commander of the Lake Erie squadron he was given the designation of commodore.

Oliver Hazard Perry and

following the XYZ affair,* and her captain, Christopher Perry, recommended his son for one of the coveted midshipman slots.

Oliver Hazard Perry was warranted a midshipman in the U.S. Navy on 7 April 1799. Over the next six years he saw active service in the Quasi-War with France and the wars against the Barbary pirates. During that period Perry sailed on such famous ships as the *General Greene, Adams, Constellation, Nautilus, Constitution,* and *Essex,* but the novice officer was not involved in any of the memorable engagements of those little known conflicts. After an extended leave in 1806-07, Perry superintended construction of a flotilla of Jeffersonian gunboats+ in Rhode Island and Connecticut, a duty he considered tedious. In April of 1809 Perry, then a 23-year-old lieutenant, finally received his first seagoing command, the 14-gun schooner *Revenge.*

Perry's vaunted good luck deserted him when he assumed command of the *Revenge.* Initially everything progressed well. During the summer of 1809 and into the following winter the *Revenge* patrolled the northeast coast of the U.S. as part of a squadron under Commodore John Rodgers. Then in the spring of 1810 Perry's ship was ordered to the Washington Navy Yard for repairs preparatory to an assignment in southern waters. But in June of 1810 the *Revenge* suffered considerable damage, including the loss of several spars,◊ after battling a severe storm while en route to her new station in Charleston, South Carolina. To make matters worse, the young lieutenant found himself plagued by illness. His fragile constitution was unable to tolerate the extreme heat and humidity of a southern summer, forcing him to request that his vessel be transferred back to northern waters.

Perry's unhappy tenure on the *Revenge* ended abruptly on 8 January 1811. Orders had been issued for the *Revenge* to conduct a survey of several harbors along the southern New England coast. Feeling her way

---

* In 1797 the French Revolutionary government, incensed at the U.S. for negotiating Jay's Treaty with England, ordered French warships to harass U.S. ships at sea. When an American diplomatic mission was sent to France, three French emissaries, dubbed X,Y, and Z, informed the U.S. mission that a payment of money might resolve the situation. The Federalists screamed bribery and corruption and called for war with France. War was averted, but a number of naval engagements occurred before the matter was settled in 1800.

+ In 1803, as a cost saving measure, Congress opted to build small coastal gunboats instead of regular warships. Between 1803 and 1811, 168 of these gunboats were built. The largest was only 75 feet long and the smallest a mere 45 feet long. Since the program was started during Thomas Jefferson's administration, the vessels were dubbed Jeffersonian gunboats.

◊ Masts, yards, gaffs, booms, etc. are all generically referred to as spars.

through the western reaches of Block Island Sound in heavy fog, the unlucky schooner struck a reef near Watch Hill Point and went down. The obligatory court-martial exonerated Perry, blaming the loss on the vessel's hapless pilot, who had assured Perry he would have no trouble navigating the sound.

Following the court-martial Perry took an extended leave of absence. On 5 May 1811 he married 20-year-old Elizabeth Champlin Mason at Newport, Rhode Island. The dashing naval officer first encountered his future bride at a dance four years earlier. An extended honeymoon was enjoyed as the newlyweds leisurely toured the New England states. Eventually the union, always described as a happy one, would produce five children, one of whom died in infancy.

Perry remained an unemployed officer until May of 1812, when the threat of war motivated the eager lieutenant to seek a new assignment. By the time war with Great Britain was declared on 18 June 1812, Perry had been ordered to assume command of the Jeffersonian gunboat squadron at Newport, the very same gunboats he helped build five years earlier. Dissatisfied with what he considered an insignificant appointment, Perry petitioned the Navy Department for a posting at sea.[12] Over the next several months, while his friends and peers were gaining glory on sleek vessels like the *Constitution*, *United States*, *Essex*, *Wasp*, and *Hornet*, Perry felt that he was being unfairly left to rot in a backwater of the war, even though he received a promotion to master commandant on 6 October 1812.[13] Unsuccessful pleas to naval authorities for an ocean-going command, including a personal interview with the Secretary of the Navy, finally prompted the disheartened Perry to expand his horizon of possibilities. Though he much preferred command of a sloop-of-war or a brig on the high seas, Perry nevertheless submitted a request for transfer to the Great Lakes to both the Navy Department and to his old acquaintance Isaac Chauncey, who then commanded naval operations on the lakes.[14]

It was this second letter that Chauncey received upon his return to Sackets Harbor from Erie on 19 January. One day later the commodore penned a reply to Perry, asserting that, "You are the very person I want for a particular service where you may gain honor for yourself and reputation for your country."[15] This was precisely what the enterprising young Perry wanted to hear. The next day Chauncey officially requested Perry's services from the Secretary of the Navy, and the anxious Rhode Islander received his new orders on 17 February. Over a period of five days Perry dispatched 150 men from the Newport Naval Station who volunteered to accompany him to the lakes, following himself immediately thereafter.

Perry first traveled to Sackets Harbor, where he met with Chauncey to discuss the situation on Lake Erie. Eager to depart for Erie forthwith, Perry was instead ordered to remain at the Lake Ontario base. The British had recently raided Ogdensburg, New York, and fearing a similar attack on Sackets Harbor, Chauncey wanted Perry by his side. Though the threat soon diminished, the cautious Chauncey prolonged Perry's stay, causing pronounced strain on Perry's part as he fidgeted to begin his new assignment. Finally, after a two-week delay at Sackets Harbor, the new Lake Erie commander received instructions to proceed to Erie.[16]

Arriving at Erie on 26 March, Perry channeled all of his energies into fitting out the new fleet. Perry often receives the lion's share of praise for completing the Lake Erie flotilla, but Isaac Chauncey was the moving force behind the fleet's construction. Much has been written about the later controversy between Chauncey and Perry over manning the fleet, a dispute that often overshadows the credit attributable to the Lake Ontario commander for his tremendous organizational abilities. Without Isaac Chauncey there would have been no powerful Lake Erie squadron. Still, such is not to say that events played out according to Chauncey's wishes, or that he magnanimously set the stage for Perry. It was never Chauncey's intention that Perry should actually command the Lake Erie squadron in battle against the British. The commodore expected Perry to supervise the flotilla's final construction, but after the vessels were completed Chauncey planned to assume command himself, leaving the junior Perry to serve as his subordinate while he personally led the Lake Erie flotilla to victory. As early as 16 March Chauncey notified the Secretary of the Navy that the ships at Erie would be ready by 1 June. By that time Chauncey also hoped that the enemy on Lake Ontario would be defeated so that he could take command on Lake Erie. Chauncey's problem was that he was never able to instigate a decisive engagement and gain naval supremacy on the lower lake.[17]

Perry, meanwhile, assumed responsibility for overseeing the myriad on-site details at Erie. Over the next two months he coped with the unrelenting practical and administrative difficulties which would arise while he struggled to build and fit a flotilla of warships in the wilderness. In 1813 Erie was a small village of only 400 people with no industrial capabilities. Items of every description were either unavailable or in short supply. The only material available in abundance was virgin timber; however, green wood had to be used since there was no time to properly cure the cut lumber, and quite often different types of wood had to be used for the same purposes. At the outset there was no iron for nails, so wooden nails, or treenails, were improvised. All other materials had to be carted in from the outside: cordage and anchors from Pittsburgh, canvas and powder from Philadelphia, and big guns from Georgetown, D.C. and New York. Even skilled laborers such as carpenters, sawyers, and blacksmiths had to be imported, some traveling a distance of 500 miles or more.[18]

Another problem for Perry was protecting the infant fleet as it was being built. When the ice on Lake Erie broke up in the spring, Presque Isle Bay and the village of Erie would be vulnerable to a naval attack or possibly even combined naval and land operations. The shallow sandbar underlying the narrow harbor entrance would slow, but not prevent a British attempt to enter the bay, and the landing of infantry on Presque Isle peninsula or on the mainland was entirely feasible. A blockhouse situated near the harbor entrance was structurally improved and more guns were added, but manpower would be required to garrison the defenses. By mid-April, Perry commanded only 60 officers and seamen plus a like number of artificers* with which to man the Erie defenses. A small measure of protection was gained when two of the new gunboats were launched. Fitted with a 12-pounder each, the schooners were anchored near the partially finished brigs, but they could provide little deterrent against a determined British attack, and manpower had to be drained from other critical operations in order to crew the gunboats.[19]

What Perry needed desperately was infantry. Fortunately for the Americans, Chauncey had foreseen this problem. On 24 February 1813, about the same time that Perry set forth from Newport, the Lake Ontario commodore informed Secretary of the Navy William Jones that a military force would be needed to protect the vessels at Erie. Jones passed the request along to John Armstrong, the newly appointed Secretary of War. Armstrong could not spare a regiment of regulars for the task, but since the vessels were being constructed in Pennsylvania, the secretary abdicated responsibility to the state's governor, Simon Snyder. Governor Snyder subsequently drafted a general order to mobilize a regiment of Pennsylvania Militia to defend the Erie squadron. The new regiment would be a provisional unit comprised of militiamen culled from several different regiments located in several different Pennsylvania counties, so the outfit would not only need time to organize and equip, but additional time to march to Erie from the central and southwestern counties of the state.[20] Due to that delay there was a period of six weeks, from late March through early

---

* The Corps of Artificers, a unit attached to the Quartermaster General's Department, comprised skilled workers and craftsmen, including master shipbuilders, carpenters, coopers, blacksmiths, etc.

May, when Erie was precariously exposed to a British attack. For their part, the British were preoccupied with the invasion of northwest Ohio and the first siege of Fort Meigs, causing them to miss a golden opportunity to attack the feebly defended base at Erie and destroy Perry's ships while they were perched on the stocks.

The British window of opportunity was slammed shut on 7 May. On that day 500 troops, half of Colonel Rees Hill's newly constituted 147th Regiment of Pennsylvania Militia, marched into Erie. Hill's remaining companies were still on the road, but would arrive within the week. Though these raw, untrained militiamen could hardly be considered an effective fighting force, their presence alone would give pause to any approaching British expedition thinking about an attack. Supplementing the infantry and bolstering the defenses were four brass 9-pounder field pieces hauled out of storage at Waterford, 15 miles below Erie.[21]

Additional reinforcements in the form of a United States Marine Corps detachment reached Erie on 17 May. Here again the credit belongs to Isaac Chauncey. On 5 March 1813, Chauncey petitioned Secretary of the Navy William Jones to have Marine Commandant Franklin Wharton dispatch a recruiting party from the Washington Navy Yard.[22] The recruiting cadre, Lieutenant John Brooks and seven rankers, departed Washington in early April. Enlistment efforts at Frederick and Hagerstown, Maryland, and Pittsburgh and Waterford, Pennsylvania, netted the leatherneck lieutenant but seven more volunteers, so that Brooks arrived at Erie with a grand total of only 15 Marines, including himself.[23]

The scion and namesake of surgeon, Revolutionary War general and later Massachusetts' governor John Brooks, the younger Brooks was born on 20 May 1783 in Medford, Massachusetts. Brooks studied medicine under the tutelage of his father after graduating from Harvard in 1805, but it was not long before he realized that medicine was not his life's calling. A military career beckoned, so Brooks sought and received a commission as a second lieutenant in the U.S. Marine Corps on 1 October 1807. He was promoted to first lieutenant on 30 January 1809. During his short career Brooks served at the Navy Yards at Boston, New York City, and Washington, D.C., and he commanded Marine detachments on U.S. Frigate *Congress* and U.S. Sloop-of-War *Wasp*. Brooks' assignment to Lake Erie in April of 1813 was not a posting for which he volunteered. In December of 1809 a court-martial board had convicted the brash young lieutenant for cheating at cards. The verdict was eventually overturned, but Brooks proved an embarrassment to Marine Corps Commandant Franklin Wharton during the long, drawn out appeals process. Chauncey's letter requesting

The Battle of Lake Erie

U.S. Marines for the Lake Erie squadron finally solved the Marine commandant's exasperating problem.[24]

The Lake Erie commander was most likely disappointed by the paltry number of leathernecks that arrived at Presque Isle, but Perry's new Marine officer was undaunted by his lack of recruiting success. Over the next eleven weeks Brooks canvassed nearby towns seeking volunteers. Other readily available sources of manpower were Hill's Pennsylvania Militia Regiment, plus the additional units from the 16th Pennsylvania Division that were eventually called up to help protect the flotilla. By the time the squadron was ready to sail in August, the resourceful Brooks had managed to enlist at least 35 more men for his Marine detachment.[25]

Perry was distracted from his manpower concerns in the latter part of May when he received word about American intentions to invade Canada once again. This time a combined land and naval force would attack Fort George, located at the mouth of the Niagara River. Leaping at the opportunity for action, the Lake Erie commodore immediately took passage for the Niagara peninsula. Perry arrived at Fort Niagara, across the river from Fort George, just in time to join Chauncey and General Henry Dearborn for the final strategy session and to secure a role in the assault, which jumped off on the morning of 27 May 1813. Perry helped align Colonel Winfield Scott's flotilla of invasion craft when they strayed off course during the initial stages of the American amphibious landing west of Fort George. After Scott's advance guard was ashore Perry boarded the schooner *Hamilton*, from which he directed a hail of grape and canister shot against British units gathering to counterattack Scott's landing force.

For Perry there was tremendous personal satisfaction in the role he played during the capture of Fort George, but even greater benefits still awaited. At the southern end of the Niagara River, just above Buffalo, lay the American naval station at Black Rock. Floating at Black Rock's wharves were five small converted gunboats. Shortly after war was declared in 1812 the navy purchased a number of small merchant vessels on Lake Erie—this was the endeavor being spearheaded by Lieutenant Jesse D. Elliott while he was corresponding with Daniel Dobbins in October of 1812. These cargo ships were sailed to Black Rock, Lake Erie's sole naval depot at the time, where their decks and supporting timbers were strengthened. They were then armed with between one and three cannons each. As warships they were relatively insignificant, but no matter how limited their potential, they were singularly needed. The only problem was that just across the Niagara River from Black Rock stood Fort Erie, and the big guns of the stone British bastion held the American naval station under a virtual state of siege. Sailing into or out of Black Rock posed an extremely hazardous risk as long as Fort Erie remained in British hands.

Hence the import of Fort George's capture. Fort George, positioned at the northern end of the Niagara River, was a major link in the supply chain to Fort Erie. When the Americans sheared that link they also severed the supply line to Fort Erie. Having no reliable source of resupply, the British were forced to abandon Fort Erie and retreat toward Burlington. Fort Erie in American hands neutralized the Black Rock blockade and released the five converted gunboats sealed there for the past seven months. Aware of these circumstances, Perry did not tarry at Fort George to receive any well-deserved accolades. Instead he rushed to Black Rock to take possession of the newly freed gunboats and prepare them for getting underway.

Two problems prevented Perry from immediately accomplishing that task: he had an insufficient number of sailors to man the converted gunboats, and he did not possess the means of moving them upriver against the Niagara River's swift current onto Lake Erie. Before setting out for Black Rock, Perry conferred briefly with Chauncey. Incredibly, the Great Lakes commander allotted his subordinate a meager two officers and 55 seamen to crew the five vessels, far too few to sail or defend even these tiny gunboats.[26]

Surprisingly it was General Dearborn who came to Perry's rescue, albeit at the behest of Chauncey. Unwilling to part with more seamen, Chauncey asked Dearborn to loan Perry 200 infantrymen. Detailed to assist Perry were two regular companies, commanded respectively by Captain Henry B. Brevoort of the 2nd United States Infantry Regiment and Captain White Young of the 15th U.S. Infantry. But even with the 200 soldiers and several teams of oxen, more than a week of grueling labor was required to fight the Niagara River's five to seven knot current in order to tow the five vessels nearly three miles upriver from Black Rock onto Lake Erie. Yet another day was lost due to adverse winds before Perry was finally able to set sail on 14 June.[27]

Once under way another serious problem faced the lightly armed flotilla. The British Lake Erie squadron was roaming the eastern basin of the lake, pining for an opportunity to engage Perry's overmatched gunboats. Endeavoring to avoid the superior enemy force, Perry hugged the New York coastline as he crept along on a southwesterly course. The voyage to Erie passed uneventfully for the Americans until, nearing his destination, Perry learned from a civilian who rowed out to warn him that the British lay in wait for the tiny flotilla near Erie. Outnumbered and hopelessly outgunned, Perry bravely cleared for action and made ready to fight.

The Battle of Lake Erie

As the five American gunboats slowly neared Erie, crews undoubtedly filled with trepidation, they were saved from certain destruction only by an anomalous trick of light and fog. Perry was to discover later that both flotillas were in sight simultaneously from land, but because of the capricious weather conditions neither was able to catch sight of the other out on the murky lake. The American vessels managed to slip past the British, and on 18 June Perry sailed into Presque Isle Bay with the Brig *Caledonia*, Schooners *Amelia*, *Ohio*, and *Somers*, and the Sloop *Trippe*.[28]

Perry now commanded 11 vessels, all of which would be armed, provisioned, and ready to sail in just a few short weeks. But the commodore's problems were far from over; developments along western Lake Erie were causing grave concern. William Henry Harrison, who was either staving off incursions by the British at Fort Meigs and Fort Stephenson or was otherwise harried by perceived invasion threats, was pressing Perry for assistance. Eager as Perry was to help his army compatriots and join the fray, there was very little he could do at this point. To be sure, the American vessels were about ready to sail, but not nearly enough seamen were available to maneuver or fight the U.S. ships. General Dearborn complicated matters by ordering the return of the 200 soldiers that he had loaned Perry to help sail the Black Rock flotilla to Erie. The only concession Dearborn made was to allow Captain Henry B. Brevoort, a resident of the Detroit region, to remain with the squadron because of his familiarity with the anticipated area of operations. After the soldiers marched off to the northeast, Perry was able to muster for his 11 vessels a mere 170 seamen. Of that number only 120 sailors were fit for duty, while the remaining 50 were consigned to the Erie station hospital, incapacitated by illness.[29]

Perry's dilemma concerning his lack of seamen was not a new one, nor was it a problem he had not been working diligently to rectify. The potential for recruiting trained seamen—or even landsmen* for that matter—in the Erie area was negligible. Several men from the town of Erie and the surrounding countryside did gravitate to the flotilla, but nowhere near the number needed to satisfy the ever-growing demands of the squadron. In order to crew his ships Perry was ultimately forced to rely upon his superior, Isaac Chauncey. Sackets Harbor served as headquarters for the Great Lakes command, and as such it was the terminus point for the large

---

* Landsmen were inexperienced recruits, newly enlisted on board ship. After a period of apprenticeship, when the novice achieved a level of knowledge and experience, he would be elevated to the next level, that of ordinary seaman.

number of seamen transferred from the East Coast to the lakes during the spring and summer of 1813. Once the reinforcements arrived at Sackets Harbor it was Chauncey's responsibility to divide those resources among his various commands.

Chauncey, though, was unable to resolve the manpower puzzle, and the roots of his quandary were firmly planted in Lake Erie. The situation on the upper lake was developing far too fast to accommodate Chauncey's original blueprint for resolving the overall British problem on the Great Lakes. Chauncey's grand scheme called first for the enemy's decisive defeat on Lake Ontario. Once the lower lake was securely in American hands, Chauncey would transfer the bulk of his officers and seamen to Lake Erie, man the ships being built at Presque Isle with his veterans from Lake Ontario, assume command of the Lake Erie squadron himself, and then defeat the British on the upper lake. But Chauncey did not, for whatever reason, bring the British to battle on Lake Ontario. Instead, naval operations on Lake Ontario evolved into a shipbuilding superiority contest, which led to tactical stalemate.

In late April, at the same time that Chauncey and Dearborn were conducting a large scale raid against York, Upper Canada (present-day Toronto), the British were invading northwest Ohio. With events unfolding so rapidly on Lake Erie, Chauncey was faced with the task of providing sufficient manpower to crew both the Lake Erie and the Lake Ontario squadrons. Cognizant of all the conflicting events and circumstances, Chauncey staunchly refused to concede his limitations and doggedly held to his original notion of defeating the enemy on both lakes himself. The longer that Isaac Chauncey clung to that inflexible attitude the more his actions would invite discord, and his chief subordinate's mercurial personality guaranteed eventual confrontation.[30]

The first ripple of the impending storm swept between Lake Erie and Lake Ontario on 9 May 1813. On that day Perry dispatched a letter to Chauncey expressing the hope that the men slated to serve on Lake Erie were on their way. Two weeks later, having received no response to his first communication, Perry attempted to prod Chauncey by suggesting that boats could be sent to Buffalo to transport sailors to Erie. Repeated efforts by Perry to solicit seamen for Lake Erie proved fruitless.[31]

As described, the commodore's initial design for the Great Lakes called first and foremost for elimination of the British squadron on Lake Ontario. Chauncey would then transfer his crews to Lake Erie, assume the mantle of responsibility and defeat the enemy on the upper lake. With this goal in mind, his procrastination in detaching men to the Erie flotilla can be attributed to his desire to retain the best seamen until the British were vanquished on Lake Ontario. Chauncey also felt, justifiably, that the Lake Erie Station would not require large numbers of sailors until the vessels under construction were nearly completed. Yet Chauncey was still preaching this unreasonable doctrine as late as 17 July, even though he knew that all of the vessels at Erie had been launched and were in the final stages of being fitted. Intelligence of British incursions into northwest Ohio in late July further crowded Chauncey's mind, as did Harrison's troubled pleas for assistance. At some point Chauncey had to realize that his original plan was no longer feasible, especially considering his lack of progress against the British on Lake Ontario. The most recent U.S. invasion of Canada, so promisingly begun on 27 May with the capture of Fort George, miscarried when the British rallied and not only attacked a superior American force at Stoney Creek on 5 June, but intimidated that poorly led army into retreating. Chauncey, meanwhile, was sparring with the British Lake Ontario squadron during the late spring and early summer, though he could not bring himself to engage the enemy in decisive battle. While Chauncey dawdled, the situation on Lake Erie was turning critical. Action was needed and needed soon.[32]

It was natural for Chauncey to be concerned with his own situation on Lake Ontario, but he was mindful that his responsibility extended to both lakes. Chauncey readily admitted and repeatedly stated that the Lake Erie command was of primary importance. He was also well aware that matters on the lower lake were not progressing according to his plan; in early June the commodore informed Secretary of the Navy Jones that it would still be some time before he would be able to leave Lake Ontario. During this same time frame Chauncey experienced few difficulties finding crews for the Lake Ontario ships. On 4 June he wrote Jones that his own vessels were "well manned and well appointed."[33] In fact, from 16 May through 10 July more than 500 reinforcements from the East Coast arrived at Sackets Harbor.[34] Until outside forces influenced him otherwise, Chauncey obstinately retained most of the men for his own fleet, forwarding only a trickle to Lake Erie. Chauncey was in agreement with both Perry and Jones that a total of 740 men were needed to crew the Erie squadron, but as mentioned, in mid-July Perry berthed only 120 men fit for duty.[35] It cannot be said that Chauncey was ignorant of the situation on Lake Erie because his correspondence with Perry and the Secretary clearly dictates otherwise.

When referring to the ensuing manpower controversy on Lake Erie, many of Perry's biographers portray chessmaster Chauncey as manipulating Perry the pawn on the Great Lakes chessboard. Viewed abstractly this image bears a measure of credence, albeit unintentionally on the part of the well-meaning Chauncey. History might have remembered Perry as a persecuted martyr at the hands of an indecisive superior had he not lost his patience and contributed to his own problem. Due to the isolated nature of the Lake Erie command, Secretary of the Navy William Jones had invited Perry to correspond directly with the Navy Department in order to keep Washington apprised of important issues. On 24 June, carrying out the Secretary's wishes, Perry updated Jones concerning activities on Lake Erie, but he added the complaint that, "The communication from Sacketts harbor [sic] to this Place occupies nearly a month, which makes it very difficult to obtain orders from Comr. Chauncey..."[36] Using these slow communications from Lake Ontario as an excuse and also lamenting his shortage of men, Perry appealed to Jones: "I shall expect your orders Sir, with great anxiety..."[37]

By going over his superior's head the Lake Erie commodore had merely taken advantage of the discretionary opportunity proffered by the Secretary of the Navy. But Perry exceeded his authority by requesting orders directly from Washington, thereby circumventing Chauncey's command prerogative. It might also be construed from Perry's letter that he was seeking to gain independence from Chauncey. Wondering why Perry importuned him for orders and curious as to what instigated this breach of military protocol, Jones immediately queried his Great Lakes commander. Chauncey, not surprisingly, was incensed by Perry's gambit and responded accordingly. After insinuating that Perry was seeking a separate command, Chauncey inquired of his subordinate, "Would it not have been as well to have made the complaint to me instead of the Secretary?" Near the end of his letter, Chauncey sarcastically added, "My confidence in Your zeal and abilities is undiminished and I sincerely hope that your success may equal your utmost wishes."[38]

Perry's transgression, inappropriate though it was, was effective nevertheless. Immediately after receiving the Secretary's missive, in which Jones tactfully suggested that a sufficient number of seamen be sent to the upper lake, Chauncey began doling out men to the Lake Erie squadron. While it was true that Perry's ploy was successful to a degree, it was at the expense of incurring Chauncey's wrath and enmity, which in turn initiated an acrimonious correspondence between the two lake commodores. That exchange of letters became so bitter and divisive that Perry was induced to submit his resignation from the Lake Erie command.

In any event, two drafts of reinforcements totaling 116 men finally arrived at Erie in late July. It soon became apparent, though, that the Lake

The Battle of Lake Erie

Erie commander was more than a little unhappy with his new shipmates. Not content to leave well enough alone, Perry again allowed his pen to get the best of him when he remonstrated to Chauncey, "The men that came...are a motley set, blacks, Soldiers and boys, I cannot think that you saw them after they were selected."[39]

Perry could not have been surprised that the different drafts of men embodied a number of African-American seamen, soldiers, or ship's boys; such a mix was common on both lake squadrons. Black sailors comprised between 10 and 20% of the complements of virtually all U.S. Navy ships and stations both before and during the War of 1812. Many of the Newport sailors who volunteered to accompany Perry from Rhode Island were black seamen. Likewise, using soldiers to help fill out crews was not uncommon. In late July, Perry and Brooks both recruited militiamen at Erie. Lastly, a review of the prize list does not reveal a disproportional number of ship's boys on board the Lake Erie squadron.[40]

What primarily disturbed the Lake Erie commodore was the fact that few of the reinforcements were trained seamen, many arrived sick and unfit for duty, and several had experienced disciplinary problems. It appeared that the best men were being retained on Lake Ontario while the dregs were being dispatched to Lake Erie. All in all, this was not an unusual practice. Chauncey most likely delegated the task of selecting men to be sent to Lake Erie, and a junior officer certainly would not pick the best seamen to be shipped to another command.[41]

Having few options, Perry accepted the debilitated soldiers and sailors, but even these men were still far from enough. In dire need of any and all manpower, Perry, like Marine Lieutenant Brooks before him, opened a recruiting station among the various Pennsylvania militia units. In addition to Hill's regiment, General David Mead had called out the entire 1st Brigade of the 16th Division in late July—the 1st Brigade was activated to augment the 147th Pennsylvania after the British squadron arrived to blockade Presque Isle Bay; the brigade remained on active duty for a period of only two weeks. From these different Pennsylvania units Perry managed to enlist approximately 65 volunteers, while Brooks found about 35 recruits for his Marine detachment.[42]

With the exception of crews, Perry's fleet was almost ready to sail, but the commodore still had two additional obstacles to overcome. Dobbins had originally selected Presque Isle Bay, among other reasons, because of its narrow, twisting, and easily guarded channel entrance. Another consideration in Dobbins' choice was the protective sand bar, lying only six feet below the surface of the channel. These impediments would prevent or disrupt any large or deep-draft British vessels from navigating the channel and destroying the American ships before they were completed. But when Dobbins chose Presque Isle he had not intended to build large 20-gun brigs; Chauncey ordered these later and caused Dobbins' good intentions to backfire. When finally launched and fitted the U.S. Brigs *Lawrence* and *Niagara* both drew nine feet of water. Further complicating matters was the lake level itself, which by 1 August had dropped, leaving only four to five feet of water over the bar. Not only could the British ships not enter the harbor, the deep draft American brigs could not get out.[43]

The impending difficulties with draft were obvious from the moment that construction of the two brigs had been authorized, and the problem inspired shipwright Noah Brown to engineer an ingenious solution. Brown designed two large rectangular barges called camels, each to be 50 feet long, 10 feet wide, 8 feet deep, and weighing 20 tons. He then instructed his foreman, Sidney Wright, to construct the awkward looking camels. For Brown's scheme to work, all guns, supplies, and portable equipment would first have to be removed from the brigs. Once lightened, a camel would be positioned on either side of one of the brigs, sunk alongside, and then by employing the anchor capstan, wooden beams through the gunports, and lines run beneath the keel, the camels would be pumped out and the brig raised just enough to slide it over the bar. Brown's complicated concoction was a masterpiece of improvisation, but timely implementation of his plan was not feasible because of the second problem: the British flotilla was lying just offshore, maintaining a careful vigil over Presque Isle Bay. Any attempt to heave the disarmed brigs over the bar could easily be smashed by the blockading British squadron.[44]

Perry's luck, holding steady from the quarter,* continued fair. On 31 July, Commander Robert Heriot Barclay's British squadron suddenly disappeared. The reasons for Barclay's unexpected departure are vague. Daniel Dobbins indicated in his writings after the war that Barclay had been invited to attend a testimonial dinner at Port Dover.[45] That such an invitation was forwarded to Barclay is certainly feasible. Still, it is reasonable to assume that Barclay abandoned his station for a more compelling reason, such as bad weather or a shortage of provisions and potable water. Another possibility is that the *Queen Charlotte* and *General Hunter* may have been damaged by American gunfire when the British tested Erie's defenses during their blockade.[46] It seems strange that a dinner invitation would be expressly issued to the British commodore while he

---

* For a sailing vessel, particularly a square-rigger, the breeze blowing from either quarter— aft of midships but not from directly astern—is this most favorable point of sailing.

was engaged in an imperative operation on the lake's opposite shore, or that a squadron commander would accept such an invitation while absorbed in a crucial assignment. Barclay was in all likelihood obliged to be at Port Dover on more pressing business, with the invitation being issued after his arrival. The matter was glossed over in his court-martial statement and, curiously, the board members did not press the issue.[47] Whatever the grounds for his actions, Barclay lifted the blockade of Presque Isle Bay at this important juncture, leaving Perry free to sail—that is, if his two brigs could clear the bar before the British returned.

Efforts to lift the brigs over the shallow sandbar at the harbor entrance were begun on 1 August. While the *Lawrence* and *Niagara* were having their guns and stores removed, the smaller gunboats sailed out to establish a picket line to protect the operation. As it turned out, dragging the first brig over the bar proved more difficult than anticipated, possibly because of the low lake level. It was necessary to elevate the cumbersome dead weight more than four feet in order to clear the bar, and the first attempt fell agonizingly short; a day of backbreaking exertion ended in failure and frustration, forcing the endeavor to be started all over again. More than 72 hours of unbelievable toil were required by every available sailor and soldier just to lug the *Lawrence* over the bar. Three long days of terrible and seemingly interminable suspense elapsed—each and every man, especially the commodore, wondering if the British warships would suddenly reappear—before the *Lawrence* floated free on Lake Erie. Many of the weary sailors and soldiers, immersed for long hours in the murky water, fell ill from the oppressive drudgery and tension.

The process was started anew with the *Niagara* and progress was rapid. Having learned some hard lessons with the *Lawrence*, the second brig required less time to heave over the bar. It appeared as if the entire enterprise would end simply and successfully. But then, on 4 August, with the *Niagara* perched high and helpless over the sandbar, British sails reappeared on the horizon.

Perry was in deep trouble. Neither of his brigs was ready to fight; the *Lawrence* was in the midst of rearming and the *Niagara* was poised, exposed and nearly out of the water, over the bar between Brown's camels. The commodore's feelings can only be imagined, but if he felt despair it was short-lived. Even though his available schooners were impossibly outgunned, Perry was not about to surrender what he worked so hard to create. Orders were quickly passed. Each of the lightly armed gunboats, in what could only be described as futile posturing, steered toward the oncoming British, screening the hamstrung brigs. Perry's situation seemed bleak. The American brigs could not possibly be made ready for action in time and the puny gunboats would do little more than provide target practice for British gunners. Odds notwithstanding, the fiery commodore was determined to go down fighting.

Amazingly, just when the American flotilla appeared doomed, Perry's luck again surged to the fore. Perceiving that his enemy's entire squadron was across the bar and being too distant to detect Perry's state of near defenselessness, Barclay assumed that his own ships were overmatched. Allowing his opponent to dodge yet another cannonball, the British commander tacked his ships around and retired toward Long Point.[48]

Perry opted to pursue Barclay as soon as the brigs could be rearmed, even though he was still alarmingly short of sailors. To help fill his ships complements the commodore again sought help from the Pennsylvania Militia. Issuing a call for fresh volunteers, at least 56 more militiamen from regiments of the 16th Division's 1st Brigade agreed to sign on for a 48-hour cruise. This additional number enabled Perry to man eight of his eleven ships, so with minimal crews he set sail after his quarry, hoping to maneuver Barclay into battle near Long Point. However, upon reaching Port Dover Perry was disappointed to find that Barclay had already weighed anchor and set sail for Amherstburg. Shorthanded and not provisioned for a long cruise, Perry wisely returned to Erie. When the American squadron dropped anchor back at Presque Isle, most of the reluctant short-time militiamen crowed that their obligation had been fulfilled. Few could be persuaded to remain with the fleet, so Perry's numbers were once again reduced.[49]

Happily for the commodore some good news awaited his return to the Erie Naval Station. Word had been received from Master Commandant Jesse Elliott that he was en route from Lake Ontario with a contingent of seamen for the Lake Erie squadron. Since Elliott's men were traveling on foot, Perry promptly dispatched the schooner *Ariel* to fetch them. Elliott soon arrived at Erie with a sorely needed 11 officers and 91 men. Even before Lake Erie's new second-in-command left Sackets Harbor, Chauncey had issued instructions to Perry that assigned Elliott as captain of the *Niagara*. Whether or not he used an extension of Chauncey's authority upon his arrival at Erie, Elliott, without consulting with his new superior, arbitrarily skimmed the cream of the fresh crewmen for his own command. Perry, pleased just to have his force augmented, chose not to challenge Elliott's questionable action and diplomatically dropped the issue.[50]

Jesse Duncan Elliott, the focal point for subsequent controversy on Lake Erie, was born in Hagerstown, Maryland in 1785. Elliott's father,

Robert Heriot Barclay

Jesse Duncan Elliott

Robert, was killed by Indians in Ohio in 1794 while serving as a Commissary Officer for the U.S. Army. In 1804, after studying law for a time in Carlisle, Pennsylvania, Elliott was warranted a midshipman in the U.S. Navy. He served on board the U.S. Frigate *Essex* during the latter stages of the Barbary pirate wars, and after his return to the United States in early 1807 Elliott was assigned to the U.S. Frigate *Chesapeake*. The timing for Elliott could not have been worse. On 22 June 1807 the *Chesapeake* was putting to sea from Norfolk, Virginia when HMS *Leopard*, a 50-gun British warship, accosted the star-crossed frigate off the Chesapeake capes. When the American ship's commander refused to turn over four sailors who the British insisted were deserters, the *Leopard* fired upon the *Chesapeake*, killing and wounding 21 of her crewmen. After the *Chesapeake* surrendered, the British captain forcibly removed the four seamen, an action that nearly precipitated war. In 1810, newly promoted to lieutenant, Elliott sailed to England on board the *John Adams*, but the small frigate had returned to the United States before war erupted in 1812.

Three months after the declaration of war Elliott was sent to Lake Erie, where he was ordered to "purchase any merchant vessels or boats that can be converted into vessels of war or gun boats, and commence their equipment immediately."[51] The Black Rock Naval Station near Buffalo was the site where Elliott would carry out those directions. At first glance Elliott's new posting did not appear to be an important assignment, but Black Rock would prove instrumental in boosting Elliott's fame and career. On the night of 8 October 1812 Elliott garnered national attention by leading a daring cutting-out expedition against two British vessels anchored off Fort Erie, just across the Niagara River from Black Rock. The brigs *Caledonia* and *Detroit** were boarded and captured by the raiding party. But as the Americans were escaping the *Detroit* ran aground and efforts to free the stranded brig proved unsuccessful. Elliott was forced to order the vessel to be abandoned and torched. Despite that substantial setback the raid was considered a huge success and it was also a valuable morale booster for the United States, not to mention the fact that it added the small brig *Caledonia* to the non-existent navy on Lake Erie. Later, when Erie, Pennsylvania was chosen over Black Rock as the shipbuilding site for Lake Erie, Elliott was reassigned to Sackets Harbor on Lake Ontario. In July of 1813, mostly due to his achievement at Fort Erie, Elliott was promoted to the rank of master commandant over 30 other lieutenants. Less than a

---

* The *Detroit* was formerly the U.S. Brig *Adams*, the only American military vessel on Lake Erie prior to the war. The *Adams* was captured when Detroit fell and the British renamed her in honor of that victory.

month later, on 3 August 1813, he received orders from Chauncey detaching him to Lake Erie.[52]

With the arrival of Elliott's contingent of seamen, Perry's squadron now billeted approximately 400 men, still an insufficient number to crew his 11 vessels. At any rate, the commodore realized that further reinforcements would not be forthcoming from Lake Ontario. Perry was becoming weary of Chauncey and his constant equivocations. It was at this point when the troubled correspondence with his superior and Secretary Jones climaxed— Perry's letter of resignation from the Lake Erie command was forwarded on 10 August.[53] No doubt exists as to Perry's resolve concerning his request for reassignment, as attested to by his transfer shortly after the battle. Nevertheless, considerable time would expire before new orders could be received, and Perry was not about to deny himself an opportunity to fight the squadron he worked so hard to man and equip. On 12 August 1813 the United States squadron set sail for western Lake Erie.

The American flotilla, ten vessels strong—the schooner *Amelia* was left at Erie—anchored off Cunningham's (Kelley's) Island four days later. Here Perry rendezvoused with William Henry Harrison, and after discussing the current state of affairs and future strategy, the commodore decided to scout his opponent's strongpoint at Amherstburg. Two reconnaissance cruises were conducted to the mouth of the Detroit River over the next two weeks, with Perry noting the presence of several British vessels lying at or near the navy yard and observing that Barclay's newly constructed flagship, was in the final stages of fitting out. No direct action on Fort Malden or the Amherstburg Navy Yard was attempted: the fort appeared to be well defended, the current in the Detroit River was swift, the winds were fickle, and there was little room for the American vessels to maneuver. Besides, there was no reason whatsoever for Perry to risk his squadron unnecessarily. The mere presence of an American naval force in the western basin of Lake Erie meant that the British would eventually have to emerge from their lair to fight.[54]

Returning to the south end of the lake, Perry received what proved to be his final reinforcements, approximately 130 soldiers from Harrison's army.[55] Precisely who originated the idea of asking for volunteers from among Harrison's regiments is uncertain, but after Perry's first meeting with the Army commander the latter circulated a general order soliciting soldiers to serve with the squadron.[56] From Fort Meigs, Fort Stephenson, and Camp Seneca they volunteered: men from the 17th U.S., 19th U.S., 24th U.S., 26th U.S., 27th U.S., and 28th U.S. Infantry Regiments, all the regular infantry units in the Northwest Army. They volunteered from Captain

Daniel Cushing's Company of the 2nd U.S. Artillery Regiment and Captain John Payne's Company of Lieutenant Colonel James V. Ball's Squadron of Light Dragoons, U.S. Volunteers. Payne's company had been a component of Colonel Richard M. Johnson's Regiment of Kentucky Mounted Volunteers, but was detached when the remainder of the regiment rode back to Kentucky to recruit and acquire fresh horses. And they volunteered from Captain Richard McRae's Company of Virginia Volunteers—the Petersburg Volunteers—from Major James Alexander's Independent Battalion.[57] For the most part only a few men were tapped from select companies of each regiment, some with prior experience on the rivers, lakes, or oceans of the world. Others appear to have been subjected to that age-old process of having a superior volunteer their services for them. Many were probably looking for adventure or a break in the routine. They soon found it.

Perry found them to be a strange bunch, but he was undoubtedly happy to see anything in the way of reinforcements, and this was not his first experience with soldiers. At least 65 men from the Pennsylvania Militia were already on board the flotilla, and the majority of Brooks' Marines had enlisted from those same Pennsylvania units. Too, numerous soldiers were scattered among the levies of reinforcements sent to Lake Erie from Sackets Harbor. Included were men from the 2nd U.S., 9th U.S., and 14th U.S. Infantry Regiments, the 1st U.S. Light Dragoons, 3rd New York Artillery, and possibly others.[58] Of the more than 550 Americans who fought in the Battle of Lake Erie, more than 40% were soldiers and Marines from more than 17 different military units located in the Lakes Erie and Ontario regions.[59]

Perry's crews were now complete. All the American flotilla commander need do at this point was bide his time at his South Bass Island base of operations, finalize planning and tactical options for the upcoming engagement, continue to train his hybrid crews of sailors, soldiers, and Marines, and wait. Perry well understood that the next move would be up to his British adversary.

The commander of the British Lake Erie squadron, Robert Heriot Barclay, was born on 18 September 1786 at King's Kettle Manse near Fife, in the Fife Region of Scotland. During the summer of 1798, at the tender age of 12, Barclay was warranted a midshipman in the Royal Navy and assigned to the gunroom on H.M. Frigate *Anson*. Barclay sat for his lieutenant's examination in December 1804 and three months later he was promoted and transferred to HMS *Swiftsure*, a 74-gun line-of-battle ship. As a junior lieutenant on board the *Swiftsure*, Barclay saw action with Lord Horatio Nelson's fleet at the cataclysmic Battle of Trafalgar on 21 October

The Battle of Lake Erie

1805. In April of 1808, while attached to H.M. Frigate *Diana*, the boyish looking officer was leading a cutting-out expedition against a French convoy anchored in Noirmoutier Roads, France when he suffered a grievous wound. The injury would cost Barclay his left arm.

Despite the loss of a limb, Barclay's naval career was not over. Gripped in a life and death struggle against Napoleonic Europe, Great Britain needed every experienced officer, even those who were partially disabled. In late 1809, barely recovered from his terrible wound, Barclay was recalled to duty and shipped to the North American Station, headquartered at Halifax, Nova Scotia. Over the next three years he saw service on H.M. Frigates *Aeolus* and *Iphigenia*. Promoted to commander in March of 1813, Barclay was sent to Lake Ontario, where he served temporarily as commanding officer of the British Lake Ontario flotilla. But Barclay's tenure with the squadron on the lower lake was all too brief. In the late Spring of 1813 Captain Sir James Lucas Yeo was appointed naval commander on Lake Ontario, whereupon Barclay was relegated to command of the British Lake Erie flotilla, but not until a more senior officer declined the Lake Erie post because of its poor state of readiness.

The British squadron on Lake Erie suffered from many of the same deficiencies as its rival, and in some areas the Scotsman's ships were even less well equipped. Barclay's superior on Lake Ontario, Sir James Lucas Yeo, was just as parsimonious with men and supplies as was Chauncey; the British squadron at Amherstburg was critically short of trained seamen. In fact, Barclay's crews were comprised mostly of soldiers from the 41st Regiment of Foot, the Royal Newfoundland Fencible* Regiment, and men from the Canadian Militia and Provincial Marine. Barclay's new flagship, the ship-rigged 19-gun *Detroit*,+ was in the final stages of fitting out, but materials of every description were simply not available. Even the cannons slated to line her broadsides failed to arrive, having been captured by the Americans on Lake Ontario. As a result, Barclay was forced to commandeer guns from Fort Malden, leaving his flagship with an undesirable amalgam of several different sizes and types of guns.[60]

Moreover, Fort Malden and the Amherstburg Navy Yard were in dire straits by the end of the first week of September. Only one narrow, rutted

---

* Fencible was a term used in the late 18th and early 19th centuries. It applied to a unit that enlisted for home service only, or for the duration of a particular conflict.

+ This vessel is the second *Detroit* to serve under the British flag in the Old Northwest. The first HMS *Detroit* was formerly the *Adams*, an American ship that the British captured when Fort Detroit surrendered. Jesse D. Elliott had retaken that vessel off Fort Erie on the night of 8/9 October 1812, but the vessel ran aground and was burned to prevent recapture.

track, grandiosely labeled the King's Road, or Detroit Road, bisected western Upper Canada between Burlington, at the southwestern edge of Lake Ontario, and Amherstburg. Supplying the massive material needs of British military operations at Fort Malden and Amherstburg over what was little better than a mud path was impossible. For this reason the British relied upon the water transportation artery across the northern reaches of Lake Erie to supply their installations on the Detroit River and the upper lakes. But the American flotilla had been criss-crossing the lake's western basin since mid-August, meaning that Perry's ships sat squarely athwart the British water supply route to Port Dover. Food stocks at the British stronghold were becoming dangerously depleted. Provisioning the military at Amherstburg was difficult enough, but in addition to British army and navy personnel, a total of 14,000 Indians in the region looked to the British for subsistence. Great Britain's Indian allies had gathered at Fort Malden from all over the Northwest, and if the British hoped to sustain their loyalty they would at the very least need to feed them. By 9 September, British storerooms at Amherstburg were reduced to a single day's supply of flour. Few options were available to General Procter and Commander Barclay. They could either defeat the American squadron to re-open their vital water supply line, or they could abandon Fort Malden, the Amherstburg Navy Yard, and the entire Western District of Upper Canada. On the afternoon of 9 September, ill prepared for battle, the British ships slipped their moorings and floated down the Detroit River onto Lake Erie.[61]

The cry of "Sail ho," bellowed by the *Lawrence*'s masthead lookout at dawn on 10 September 1813, provoked a flurry of activity. Dulaney Forrest, *Lawrence*'s second lieutenant, hurried a messenger below to inform the commodore. Within minutes American crewmen were scurrying about the deck and scrambling into the rigging, making preparations to get underway.[62] The time at Put-in-Bay had been well spent with planning and training, though one worrisome factor was a debilitating "lake fever" that was running rampant among Perry's crews; the commodore himself had been confined to his cabin for a time. On the morning that the American squadron sailed into battle, 116 men were recorded as unfit for duty due to illness, about 20% of Perry's total complement.[63]

But Perry was not about to miss his great opportunity. By 0600 the American squadron of nine vessels was under sail and working to windward—the schooner *Ohio*, commanded by Daniel Dobbins, had been ordered to Erie for supplies a few days earlier and subsequently missed the engagement.[64] According to the previously developed order of battle, the *Niagara* preceded the *Lawrence* out of Put-in-Bay. Assuming that Barclay

The Battle of Lake Erie

would post the *Detroit* in the middle of the British battle line for the purpose of command and control, Perry had placed his own flagship accordingly. Perry's attack plan otherwise specified which British ship each U.S. vessel would engage, so the American squadron sailed out of Put-in-Bay in the order of battle dictated by the commodore's predetermined tactics.[65] The American fleet bore up by Gibralter Island and moved out to meet the British.

Whenever the Battle of Lake Erie is discussed, or for that matter any naval action of this time period, two fundamental factors must be considered. First is the type of cannon in use. The preponderance of artillery pieces on board the British Lake Erie squadron were long guns, the standard naval cannon of the day that could accurately fire a cannonball approximately one-half mile. The Americans, however, followed a different philosophy, and with the exception of a 12-pounder bow chaser* in each broadside, Perry's two large brigs were armed with carronades. A relatively recent invention, the carronade possessed several advantages over the traditional long gun: it could be loaded and fired at a faster rate, required fewer gun crewmen, was more economical to operate since it used less powder, was more accurate, and fired a much heavier cannonball than a long gun of comparable weight—a 32-pounder carronade barrel weighed less than a 12-pounder long gun tube. Nonetheless, the carronade suffered from one significant disadvantage; it had less than half the effective range of a long gun of similar caliber.[66]

The second factor is the wind. Most large ships of the period were square-rigged sailing vessels. A square-rigger has square-shaped sails lashed to yards which, when rigged to a mast, are perpendicular to the axis of the ship, as opposed to a schooner or sloop, which has sails rigged fore and aft on the same axis as the ship. The yards on a square-rigger can be pivoted, or braced around, to take full advantage of the wind, but movement of the yards is limited and a square-rigger can not sail into the eye of the wind or within an arc of roughly 145° of the wind's direction. A sailor's compass is apportioned equally into 32 points, 16 per side or, divided into quarters, eight points forward and aft of the ship's beam. For a square-rigger to make headway steering a steady course, the wind could not be more than two points forward of the ship's beam, the maximum

---

* Cannons were classified by the weight of the cannonballs they fired. Simply put, a 12-pounder fired a 12-pound shot. Bow-chasers were the forward-most guns on the gun deck. Regardless of how a ship was armed, a long gun would be mounted in the bow for additional reach in the event that one vessel ended up chasing another.

angle that the yards could be braced around to catch the breeze. When two ships, or two squadrons in this instance, were engaged in battle, the one with the wind behind it held the weather gauge, or wind advantage.

As Perry's squadron rounded Gibralter Island that morning his vessels stood to the westward. The reason for Perry's sailing point was the wind, which was blowing lightly from the southwest, a direction that awarded Barclay the advantage of the weather gauge. In order to steal the weather gauge Perry would have to sail to a point west of Rattlesnake Island; he could then turn to the northwest and have the wind off his larboard* beam. Attempting to achieve his objective, Perry started beating into the wind, repeatedly tacking back and forth in a zigzag pattern between Rattlesnake and South Bass Island, trying to make headway. The wind, though, was light and variable, and the shallow-draft brigs were making too much leeway; the larger American vessels simply lacked the necessary sailing qualities to fore reach to windward. After more than three hours of exhausting and frustrating labor, Perry finally yielded to nature's forces and ordered Sailing Master William V. Taylor to wear ship[+] and bear down to the northeast. Perry's intention was to fight the battle either among or to the eastward of the islands. Taylor objected to his commodore's bidding, aware that such a maneuver would defer the wind advantage to the British. "I don't care," Perry testily rebuffed Taylor's advice, "to windward or to leeward, they shall fight today."[67]

At four bells in the forenoon watch (1000 hours), Taylor had just passed the order to put the helm up when, remarkably, Perry's luck again rose to the fore. Even before Taylor could execute the commodore's order the wind suddenly shifted, backing between 60° to 90° and blowing variably from the southeast, bestowing the critical advantage of the weather gauge upon the American squadron. With the wind now at his coattails, Perry aimed his bowsprits in a northwesterly direction, straight for the British fleet. Barclay, the weather gauge lost and having limited options, wore around to the west and hove to[◊] to await his adversary.

---

* In early naval terminology larboard was left and starboard was right; however, the terms were understandably confusing and larboard was eventually changed to port, but in 1813 larboard was still the accepted usage.

+ To wear ship means to turn with the wind, whereas to tack means to maneuver by turning into the wind.

◊ Heave to is a general term that can mean to make headway slowly, to stop dead in the water, or to make sternway. The evolution is carried out by counter-bracing one or more of the ship's yards in order to back one or more sails, and by issuing variable helm orders.

The Battle of Lake Erie

As the British line wore around, Barclay's tactical dispositions were disclosed to the Americans for the first time. Perry now discerned that his assumption concerning the placement of Barclay's flagship was in error. Rather than locate his largest ship in the center of his squadron as Perry had anticipated, Barclay had placed the *Detroit* in the second slot in his line. Should Perry wish to adhere to his own previously established tactical plan it would be necessary for him to adjust the American battle line. But before making any changes Perry passed instructions for the *Niagara* to heave to so that the *Lawrence* could creep up alongside. Through a speaking trumpet the commodore conversed with Captain Henry B. Brevoort, commander of the *Niagara*'s makeshift Marine detachment, to make certain that his assessment of the British battle line was accurate. Brevoort was an army captain and resident of the Detroit region who, prior to the war, commanded a supply vessel on Lake Erie and was thus familiar with and could easily recognize most of the enemy vessels.[68]

Finding that his analysis of the enemy was sound, the commodore proceeded to reorganize his own line of battle. As per his original plan, Perry left the schooner *Scorpion*, with two heavy guns, and the schooner *Ariel*, carrying four light artillery pieces, positioned slightly off the squadron's weather bow.* From this location the two schooners could engage Barclay's leading vessel and dissuade the British from crossing in front of the Americans in order to rake+ their line. Opposite these two gunboats was the schooner *Chippawa*, which was the first British vessel in line and mounted but one cannon. Perry's 20-gun flagship *Lawrence* now ranged ahead of the *Niagara* to the third position in line to combat Barclay's flagship, the 19-gun *Detroit*; by this action Perry removed Elliott from the American van, the so-called point of honor. The *Caledonia*, a smallish brig with three heavy guns, followed astern of the *Lawrence* and was designated to fight the *General Hunter*, a little brig mounting 10 light-caliber guns. Placed fifth in the American line was the *Niagara*, Perry's other 20-gun brig and a sistership of the *Lawrence*. The *Niagara* would close with the *Queen Charlotte*, a 17-gun ship-rigged vessel and Barclay's second largest

---

* The weather side was the portion of the ship across which the wind was blowing. At this point of the Battle of Lake Erie, with the wind blowing generally from the southeast and Perry's ships steering a course slightly west of northwest, the wind was blowing across the Americans' left rear, or larboard quarter. The weather side of the *Lawrence* was the larboard side, and the weather bow was off the larboard, or left front of the ship.

+ Raking fire, the ultimate tactical evolution in a naval battle, occurred when a warship sailed either in front of or astern of another vessel. The raking warship, assuming a position perpendicular to the other ship, was able to fire all of its guns on the engaged side while the vessel being raked was unable to respond. This maneuver was called crossing the "T."

warship. Lastly for Perry came the gunboats *Somers*, *Porcupine*, *Tigress*, and *Trippe*, with each mounting one or two heavy guns. These smaller American vessels were assigned to battle Barclay's last two ships, the schooner *Lady Prevost*, with 13 light guns and the sloop *Little Belt*, mounting three small cannons (see Appendix A for a listing of warships and armament).

Altogether the six British vessels that fought in the engagement mounted 35 long guns and 28 carronades, conferring upon Barclay a combined broadside strength* of about 460 pounds. Conversely, the nine American vessels that Perry committed to battle incorporated 15 long guns and 39 carronades, with an aggregate broadside volume of 924 pounds, double that available to Barclay. The British did possess a significant numerical advantage in long guns, 35 as opposed to 15, but in a battle employing guns arrayed in broadside—in parallel lines perpendicular to the axis of the ship—it was broadside power that counted, and broadside weight usually ordained a battle's outcome. Perry's more numerous and heavier caliber carronades endowed the Americans with a tremendous firepower advantage. The large 32-pounder smashers, heaving a six-inch diameter ball, gave Perry a massive 664 to 288 pound broadside advantage in carronades.[69]

The smaller vessels of each squadron would not play a vital role in the battle. Both commanders understood that the four larger square-riggers would decide the outcome. Almost all of Perry's 32-pounder carronades squatted on his two 20-gun brigs. The *Lawrence* and *Niagara* each mounted eighteen 32-pounder carronades on their single gun decks plus two 12-pounder long guns as bow chasers. Her heavy carronades invested the *Lawrence* with a broadside variance of 300 pounds over the *Detroit*'s 138 pounds, while the *Niagara*'s broadside weight exceeded the *Queen Charlotte*'s by 300 pounds to 192 pounds—the latter carried fourteen 24-pounder carronades. Thus if the *Lawrence* could close with the *Detroit* and the *Niagara* could converge on the *Queen Charlotte*, then Perry would retain a decided advantage with his much heavier carronades.[70] Barclay's best hope in such an unequal contest would be to either cripple the sailing

---

* Broadside strength is the total weight of metal fired by a ship's or squadron's guns from the engaged side. Using the *Lawrence* as an example, if all ten guns in her broadside were 32-pounders and all fired at the same time, she would amass a broadside strength of 320 pounds. If the *Detroit* had ten guns per side and all fired at the same time, but they were only 18-pounders, then that vessel would have a broadside strength of 180 pounds. The larger the guns, the greater the advantage.

capabilities of one or both of the American brigs before they closed within carronade range, or somehow inflict enough damage that the American carronades would not play a decisive role.

The wind shift had transferred the advantage to the Americans. Perry could now dictate the distance at which the engagement would be fought, and the Americans could more easily initiate offensive tactical maneuvering instead of simply responding defensively to aggressive moves, as would Barclay. But the breeze was light, meaning it would require considerable time for Perry to close within range of the British.

In an effort to animate his crew and divert their attention from the demoralizing wait, the American commander chose this interval to hoist his new battle flag to the topmast of the *Lawrence*. It was a large blue banner crudely inscribed in white letters with the words "DONT GIVE UP THE SHIP." Often attributed to Perry himself, this phrase was actually the dying declaration of a friend of Perry's, Captain James Lawrence. Lawrence was mortally wounded on 1 June 1813 when his ship, the U.S. Frigate *Chesapeake*, dueled the British frigate *Shannon* off Cape Ann, Massachusetts. Below deck and in terrible pain after being struck by a musket ball in the groin, Lawrence was informed that his ship was lost. According to one version Lawrence angrily retorted, "...keep the guns going and fight the ship till she sinks...Don't give up the ship. Blow her up."[71] Ironically, Lawrence's men did surrender, and in record time; the battle between the *Chesapeake* and the *Shannon* was one of the briefest and most deplorable actions in all of American naval history. Even so, Perry's flagship was named for his dead friend and Lawrence's dying utterance was embraced as Perry's battle slogan. The words hardly inspired confidence, having a negative connotation, but if nothing else they clearly indicated Perry's determination to do his utmost in the coming engagement.

And now, as the American warships crept ever so slowly closer to the British line, there was nothing for the crews to do but wait. Every sailor who had ever fought in a close-quarters naval engagement knew what to expect, and those who had not were blithely ignorant of the carnage that awaited. The experienced seamen of both squadrons were aware that a naval fight embodied more terror and unleashed more horror than a land battle ever could. It was not just cannonballs that these battle-hardened veterans feared, though solid iron balls weighing, depending upon the caliber of the gun, between 4 and 32 pounds, were certainly intimidating enough. They were afraid of wood splinters, because when a cannonball plowed into the side of a wooden ship the planking and framing would shatter and showers of splinters, ranging in size from a fingernail to a boarding pike,* scoured the deck. They were afraid of grape shot, canister shot, chain shot, bar shot, langrage,+ and anything else that could belch from the throat of a smoothbore cannon. They were afraid of being raked, where a single cannonball carved a path of devastation the entire length of an open-decked ship crammed with humanity. They were afraid of severed spars and rigging falling from aloft, or cannons tossed askew or overturned by enemy shot, all of which could crush and maim. They were afraid of muzzle flashes or sparks igniting tinder dry wood and canvas, fire always being the sailor's nemesis. They were afraid of being forced into the water since most sailors never learned how to swim. They were afraid of being boarded, where savage hand-to-hand fighting entailed personal bloodletting and mutilation with musket, pistol, bayonet, cutlass, boarding axe, boarding pike, dirk, belaying pin, sponge-rammer, handspike, and even hands, feet, and teeth if necessary. But most of all they were terrified of being wounded and having to face the dank horror of the orlop deck, where the surgeon awaited in his bloodspattered butcher's apron with probes, forceps, scalpels, and bone saws, with a shot of rum or whiskey◊ as the only anesthetic and a leather strap or musket ball shoved between the wounded man's teeth to choke off the screams as shipmates securely pinned flailing arms and legs to the gory operating table. Seaman David Bunnell of the *Lawrence* described the waiting as:

> ...a time to try the stoutest heart. My pulse beat quick—all nature seemed wrapped in awful suspense—the dart of death hung as [if] it were trembling by a single hair, and no one knew on whose head it would fall.[72]

Unlike the wind, Perry's luck had held steady so far, but he began to encounter problems prior to entering within range of the British guns. His sternmost vessels were having difficulty keeping up with the leading ships. The light wind at this time was inconsistent and variable, the fluky breeze preventing the trailing gunboats from maintaining their station. With

---

* A boarding pike is a spear-like weapon used mostly to repel enemy boarders. In the War of 1812 the pike staff averaged eight to nine feet in length, while the metal triangular-shaped pike head was about 16 inches long.

+ Langrage, or langridge, is a multi-purpose cannon round used against sails and rigging, or against personnel. A langrage round is easily and simply made by sewing scrap pieces of iron, nails, or similar materials into a pocket of canvas.

◊ Unlike the Royal Navy, which issued rum to ships' crews, the U.S. Navy preferred whiskey. Since it was made from native U.S. grain, whiskey was deemed more appropriate for American sailors than West Indian-distilled British rum.

sweeps* working and all sail set these little ships still could not add knots. Before the first shot was even fired the American squadron had broken into two separate divisions, the smaller vessels bringing up the rear of Perry's line as much as two miles astern of the first five ships. Choosing to allow the struggling gunboats to catch up as best they could, Perry pressed ahead toward the British line.

At 1145 a bugle sounded on board the *Detroit*. Musicians on the British flagship then played "Rule Britannia," which was immediately followed by the blast of a 24-pounder long gun, a ranging shot which splashed harmlessly near the *Lawrence*. A few minutes later a second 24-pounder was fired, but this time the ball smashed through the *Lawrence*'s starboard bulwark and flying splinters killed and wounded American sailors. The range was still too great for the *Lawrence*'s carronades, so Perry ordered the *Scorpion*, with one long 32-pounder, and the *Ariel*, with four long 12-pounders, to open fire. The *Caledonia* let loose with her long 24's, and the *Lawrence* added her long 12-pounder bow chaser to this opening exchange.[73]

Immediately after the British opened fire, Perry hoisted a signal for his ships to engage as they came up, each vessel to fight its designated opponent as specified in previously issued orders.[74] The Americans had been closing at an angle of about 15°, but Perry now ordered the flagship's helm to be put up in order to close swiftly to carronade range. The commodore chose to make as rapid an approach as possible at a fairly sharp angle, even though that decision exposed the American flotilla to a raking fire from the British long guns; no matter which approach Perry selected, the American ships would be under fire from Barclay's long guns until the range shortened. Closing in this manner, only a few American long guns could be brought to bear to answer the British broadsides. In frustration, or in an attempt to distract his crews' attention from the deadly British fire, Perry luffed+ the *Lawrence* and loosed a broadside with his carronades, but the balls plummeted into the water well short of the British ships. There was nothing for Perry to do except to put the helm up once again, bear down on the enemy line, and absorb the punishment until his short-range carronades could take effect.[75]

Finally, at 1215, the *Lawrence* edged into range and Perry again luffed his flagship, but this time the heavy 32-pound balls from his broadside crashed into the British ships. Having sailed to within carronade range, the

---

* Smaller sailing ships carried large oars, or sweeps, to aid propulsion when the wind failed. Even the big American brigs could deploy sweeps.

+ To turn a vessel into the wind without changing tack.

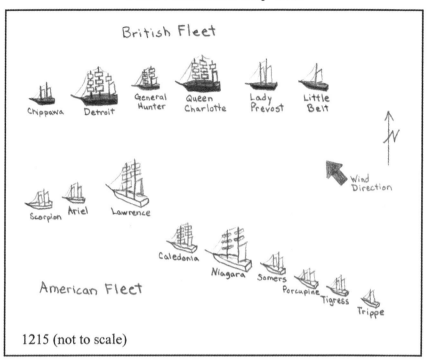

1215 (not to scale)

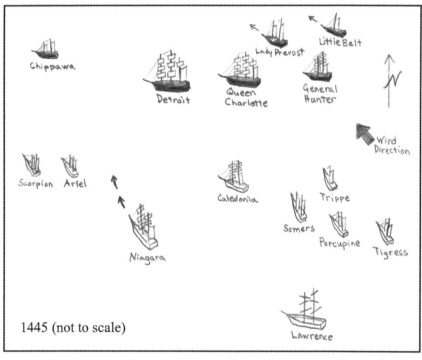

1445 (not to scale)

The Battle of Lake Erie

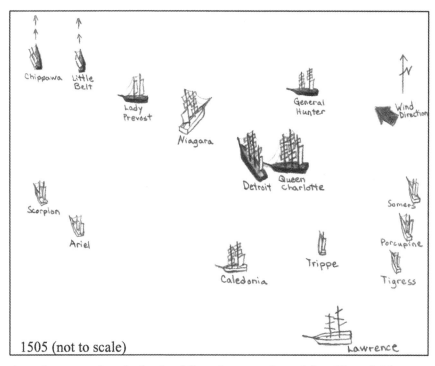

1505 (not to scale)

American squadron had seized the advantage in weight of broadsides—at least it would as soon as the *Niagara* closed with the *Queen Charlotte*, after which the battle's outcome should only be a matter of time.

But it was not to be! Peering astern, fully expecting to see the *Niagara* crowding forward into supporting distance of the flagship, Perry was dismayed to note that Elliott had instead brailed* up the *Niagara*'s jib and backed her main topsail. Elliott's sail handling not only arrested the *Niagara*'s forward motion, but also stalled her out of range of the *Queen Charlotte*'s 24-pounder carronades. The steady bark of *Niagara*'s starboard bow chaser could be heard, and Elliott had even ordered the larboard 12-pounder to be rolled across to fill the empty forward gun port to starboard, but the brig's carronades were still well out of range.[76]

Extenuating circumstances for Jesse Elliott's inertia did exist. When Perry conveyed his battle plan to his subordinates prior to the engagement, he issued two specific orders that would eventually prove to be somewhat contradictory in nature. Perry's first mandate was: "Commanding officers are particularly enjoined to pay attention in preserving their stations in the

---

* Brails are lines used to furl fore and aft sails.

Line, and in all cases to keep as near the *Lawrence* as possible."[77] During the age of fighting sail the line of battle—ships following each other single file with very little distance between vessels—was a rigid tactic. Two opposing lines of battle would close within range of the great guns and blaze away until the enemy either withdrew, surrendered, or an opportunity presented itself where the damaged opponent could be boarded and captured. If a ship's captain was to arbitrarily veer away and leave a gap in the line of battle, an alert and aggressive enemy could maneuver through that gap to rake his antagonist's line with one or both broadsides. While naval strategists were beginning to reconsider that unyielding tactic, especially in light of Horatio Nelson's innovations before his death at Trafalgar in 1805, at the time of the War of 1812 a warship commander would disrupt his own line of battle only at the risk of losing the engagement, command of his ship, and his career.

The second instruction received by American vessel commanders was to "Engage each your designated adversary, in close action, at half cable's* length."[78] As the fighting intensified, the tactical situation evolved to a point where the *Niagara*'s commander would find difficulty fulfilling his orders.

The *Caledonia*, with only three guns—two long 24-pounders and a 32-pounder carronade, all on pivot+ mounts—and posted directly ahead of the *Niagara*, was first to shorten sail. Completely outclassed, the *Caledonia* would have been no match for the *Queen Charlotte*'s fourteen 24-pounder carronades and three 12-pounder long guns had she closed within carronade range, so Lieutenant Daniel Turner's decision to slow the *Caledonia* was reasonable. Justification for the *Niagara* to shorten sail had thus been furnished because at this point Elliott was simply following Perry's order to preserve his station in line.

Elliott eventually realized, after an unspecified interval, that his ship was ineffective in its present position. As long as his brig remained motionless astern of the *Caledonia*, an ever-widening gap was separating the *Niagara* from the flagship and the British, who were maintaining a measure of forward motion. The wind for the British was foul, so Barclay

---

* A cable length is a nautical measure of distance: 120 fathoms (720 feet) in the British Navy, and 100 fathoms (600 feet) in the U.S. Navy.

+ Pivot mounts are usually located on the centerline of a warship and are designed so that they could swivel, or pivot, to fire off either side of the ship. If the warship had no bulwarks, as was the case with some of the American gunboats, then the gun would have a wide arc of fire.

The Battle of Lake Erie

could not exploit the gap and maneuver to rake the American battle line, and Elliott had to know that his vessel was serving no purpose whatsoever while it remained out of carronade range. Possibly in an attempt to close within carronade range, Elliott issued orders for the *Niagara* to again gather way and pass the *Caledonia* to windward. After this point, however, Elliott's actions are uncertain and a matter of considerable controversy to this day. Regardless of what orders Elliott delivered after leaving the *Caledonia* astern, most contemporary accounts corroborate that the *Niagara* did not, as directed, engage its designated adversary in close action, or even draw within carronade range of the *Detroit* or *Queen Charlotte* until after Perry shifted his flag from the *Lawrence* around 1430. *Niagara*'s officers later supported their captain and testified that the brig was in close action early in the battle, but the other officers of the squadron disagreed, and Purser Samuel Hambleton, a Perry advocate, stated that Elliott's ship did not even sail within long gun range of the enemy.[79]

Whether or not Jesse Elliott was derelict in his duty is debatable. For the sake of posterity, the *Niagara*'s commander supplies abundant grist for the historians' mill, but in the short term the motives for Elliott's behavior had little relevance, what mattered was the outcome of his actions. Already deprived of the wayward gunboats' long guns, the loss of *Niagara*'s carronades abruptly reduced Perry's effective broadside strength by an additional 37%, leaving the commodore to fight with less than half of his overall firepower.[80]

Losing the *Niagara*'s weapons was not the only repercussion that stemmed from Elliott's lack of activity. The *Niagara* was slated to engage the *Queen Charlotte* at close range. Now, having no American combatant within range of his ship's 24-pounder carronades and desiring to place his battery where it would have the greatest effect, the *Queen Charlotte's* commander spread additional sail and forged ahead of the *General Hunter*; the *Queen Charlotte*'s broadside was then trained upon the *Lawrence*. At this point in the engagement, with the *Niagara* some distance astern and, by most accounts, out of carronade range, the *Detroit* and *Queen Charlotte* were concentrating on the *Lawrence*, while the *General Hunter* also lobbed intermittent broadsides at the American flagship. The *Lawrence* would remain as the enemy's focal point and continue to endure the unceasing onslaught of British firepower for the next two interminable hours.

In naval fiction one occasionally encounters the melodramatic phrase, "the decks ran red with blood." In the case of the *Lawrence* on that bloody afternoon of 10 September 1813, fact supplanted fiction. Marine Lieutenant John Brooks was straddling the quarterdeck near Perry when a

41

cannonball slammed into his side, shattering his pelvis and carrying away most of his hip joint and part of his thigh. Incapable of enduring the vicious pain, Brooks pleaded with the commodore to end his misery, but Perry could not bring himself to kill his comrade. Brooks was eventually carried below deck where, after more than an hour of excruciating suffering, he finally died.[81] Boatswain's Mate William Johnson was struck on the chest by grapeshot.* Most likely fired from long range, the grapeshot had apparently lost most of its velocity because it did not penetrate; instead it bounced off Johnson's chest. Nonetheless, the iron sphere retained enough momentum to break three of Johnson's ribs.[82] A wood splinter pierced Marine Private David Christie's shoulder, plowed a ragged furrow through his torso, and came to rest near his hip joint.[83] Another Marine Private, Samuel Garwood, was bashed on the back of his head and shoulders by a falling backstay block. The heavy wooden block clubbed Garwood to the deck, blood and other matter trickling from his ears.[84]

British roundshot and grapeshot gouged saw-toothed holes through the *Lawrence*'s bulwarks with distressing frequency, launching showers of deadly wood splinters. The iron projectiles and wood splinters decimated the flagship's crowded gundeck. A British shot mashed the head of a gunner standing near Seaman David Bunnell. The man's brains were sprayed so thickly in his face that Bunnell was temporarily blinded. Once the horrified Bunnell was assured that the brains were not his own he continued to serve his carronade.[85] A piece of shrapnel slashed through Seaman John Newen's tarred hat and penetrated his skull; the unconscious Newen was carried below to the surgeon.[86] Carpenter's Mate George Cornell was also struck on the head just above his temporal bone.[87] Quartermaster's Mate Francis Mason and Seaman James Miles both suffered a compound fracture to the left humerus within two inches of the shoulder, while Ordinary Seaman John Schrouder had his right arm nearly ripped off.[71] Seaman William Thompson suffered a dangerous wound to his left leg, and Seaman John Burdeen, Seaman Andrew Mattison, Seaman George Varnum, Ordinary Seaman Charles Van Dyke, and Ordinary Seaman Jeremiah Easterbrook were all severely wounded in the right leg.[88]

As casualties mounted, fewer and fewer men were available to serve the guns. Sailors and soldiers alike were forced to fill in wherever they

---

* Grapeshot was an anti-personnel projectile that derived its name because its three-tiered shape resembled a bundle of grapes. The round split apart when fired from a cannon and, depending upon the caliber of the shot, scattered grape-sized to plum-sized iron balls like a shotgun blast. 24-pounder grapeshot of the type fired from the British ships incorporated nine 32-ounce shot.

were needed, and Marines were ordered to stow their muskets and fill in the ever-increasing gaps at the carronades. Purser Samuel Hambleton, assigned to supervise a section of two carronades, later wrote:

> I lost several of my little command, & at length, being told, on application, that I could not have any more men & finding that both guns could not be managed without another hand; I laid hold myself. Capt. Perry observing this ordered all the officers to work at the guns.[89]

Purser Hambleton performed admirably until, as he remembered, "...I had my left shoulder-blade broke [sic] by something from aloft which struck me down, tore the clothes from my back, and bruised me dreadfully."[90]

Acting Master's Mate Thomas Claxton was less fortunate than Hambleton. The youthful Claxton, son of the doorkeeper to the House of Representatives, was considered one of the most promising officers in the squadron. Claxton, like Hambleton, was struck on the shoulder; not by something from aloft, but by a cannonball, and the ball was not spent. The solid iron sphere "carried away all the bones of the [shoulder] joint, the clavicle, scapula and head of the humerus.[91]

One by one the men of the *Lawrence* were cut down, and one by one they either crawled or were helped below deck for treatment by the surgeon. But if the wounded had hoped for safety and comfort they were sorely disappointed, because the situation below was little better than the bloodbath they just left on the gundeck. Normally in a ship of war the sick bay, or the surgeon's operating area, was situated below the waterline where the wounded were protected from projectiles penetrating the vessel's side. Such was not the case with the *Lawrence*. The American flagship was a shallow-draft vessel built to navigate and fight over the shallow depths of western Lake Erie; consequently the *Lawrence*'s wardroom, located just below the main deck and above the waterline, was converted into an improvised operating theater.

The *Lawrence*'s surgeon, Samuel Horseley, was disabled by fever, so 25 year-old Surgeon's Mate Usher Parsons assumed the duties of acting-surgeon. Parsons, along with six helpers detailed to carry the wounded below or to restrain them during surgery, coped with the steady stream of horrors that flowed below from the flagship's blasted gundeck. Even as Parsons operated, cannonballs crashed through the starboard bulkhead of the wardroom, one passing only a few inches over his head. At one point Parsons had just finished fixing a splint on the arm of Midshipman Henry Laub. Laub's arm had been flayed open and badly fractured by a wood splinter. Parsons was in the process of telling Laub to go forward and lie down—he still had his hand on the youngster's arm—when a cannonball burst through the bulkhead and drove into Laub's side, flinging the midshipman's "half severed" body to the deck, a shapeless bloody bundle.[92] Seaman Charles Pohig, a Narragansett Indian, was treated for two broken arms and then placed on deck to rest. Before long another ball breached the bulkhead and ripped through both of the wretched seaman's legs. Pohig lasted another hour before expiring.[93]

Some grim humor did materialize to lighten the gory drama in the wardroom. John Yarnall's head and face were smeared with blood from a severe scalp wound. The first lieutenant, choosing duty over the surgeon's ministrations, did not immediately go below for treatment. He was near the foremast overseeing the firing of the first division's guns when a cannonball punched through the hammock nettings. A miniature cloudburst of flag bunting and cattails showered the deck, with some of the shredded bunting and cattails adhering to Yarnall's sticky face. When he eventually went below to have his lacerated scalp and another injury treated, a few of the wounded thought that the grotesque sight of Yarnall's bloodied and splotched face "made his head resemble that of a huge owl." Several of the wounded sailors laughed and shouted that the devil had finally come to get them.[94]

As his surgery became increasingly crowded, Parsons suddenly heard his name being called. Peering up through the wardroom skylight, the surgeon could see Perry on the main deck above. With his gun crews largely depleted, the commodore was compelled to order Parsons to send one of his assistants on deck to help fight the ship. Repeatedly this scenario was played out until all six of Parsons' assistants had departed. Finally, Perry resorted to asking if any of the wounded or seriously ill were capable of joining the fight, and those few that could still function stumbled or crawled on deck to do what little they could. Carpenter's Mate Wilson Mays, who had been sick before the battle, volunteered to man the bilge pumps. After the engagement Mays was found still at his post, a British sharpshooter's musket ball through his heart.[95]

The *Lawrence* was not the only U.S. warship to incur casualties during the tumultuous exchange of broadsides. Off the flagship's weather bow, Sailing Master Stephen Champlin's *Scorpion* and Lieutenant John Packett's *Ariel* added their guns to the fray. While not the focus of British attention, the schooners did not escape. On board the *Scorpion*, Pennsylvania Militia private William Hight suffered a slight wound to his left calf, but his situation worsened only moments later when his left kneecap was sheared off.[96] Midshipman John Clark was killed instantly when a cannonball

The Battle of Lake Erie

Usher Parsons

John J. Yarnall

Samuel Hambleton

Stephen Champlin

pulped his head.[97] Also killed on the *Scorpion* was militia private John Silhammer, a saddler from Centre County, Pennsylvania.[98]

Long 12-pounders from the *Ariel*'s gundeck lashed out at the enemy, and the British responded in kind. Landsman William Sloss was prostrated when a wood splinter penetrated his chest.[99] Pennsylvania militiaman John Lucas was helping to crew one of the *Ariel*'s 12-pounders. Not thoroughly versed with the workings of naval cannon, Lucas stood too close to the rear of the gun when it discharged. When the cannon recoiled, the 12-pounder's heavy wooden truck* rolled over Lucas's foot, crushing his toes. Recoiling to its limit, the cannon slammed against its breech rope+ and rebounded forward; before anyone could move to assist the hapless Lucas his foot was crunched a second time.[100]

In the midst of the cannonade, one of the *Ariel*'s apparently overloaded 12-pounders discharged prematurely. The recoil was so severe that the tube leapt off its carriage. Private William Smith of the 26th U.S. Infantry was a gun crewman manning the 12-pounder's side tackle. Smith, in the process of hauling on the tackle to roll the gun back into battery, neglected to release the three-quarter inch manila rope when the gun fired. The rapidly running line burned through the flesh, muscle, and sinew on both of his hands.[101] Standing by the *Ariel*'s tiller during the entire engagement was Pilot Asel Wilkinson. At one point Wilkinson felt a tug at his side. Looking down, the veteran mariner discovered that a British cannonball had ripped off the cartridge box he had been wearing. Wilkinson remained steadfastly at his duty station despite the dull red streaks of blood streaming from his nose and ears due to the pealing bark and mind numbing concussion of *Ariel*'s 12-pounder long guns.[102]

Astern of the *Lawrence*, the *Caledonia* blazed away with her two 24-pounder long guns—the small brig probably did not close within range to use her single 32-pounder carronade. A number of British cannons were also leveled at the *Caledonia*; three men were wounded on the brig and a fourth was injured in an accident. The latter occurred when Carpenter's Mate Isaac Peckham's leg was partially crushed when it became jammed between a gun carriage and one of the masts when the big 24-pounder recoiled.[103]

Although the British tossed an occasional shot at the gunboats supporting the *Lawrence*, the flagship swallowed the bulk of the British

---

* The solid wooden wheels on naval gun carriages were called trucks.

+ Most naval cannons had an iron ring (breech ring) affixed to the rear section (cascable) of the barrel. A heavy rope, attached to the ship's bulwark by a ring bolt on either side of the gun, passed through the breech ring and was used to absorb the cannon's recoil.

squadron's offerings. The guns of the *Lawrence* were systematically silenced until finally, only one cannon, possibly the aftmost carronade on the starboard side, was left firing. Perry himself pitched in to help the gun's crew until this last carronade was also incapacitated. With all of her starboard guns disabled and deprived of the ability to maneuver, the tortured flagship was finished as a fighting ship.

By five bells in the afternoon watch (1430), the *Lawrence* was a floating, helpless wreck: sails were pockmarked and hung limply in tattered strips; rigging trailed from her masts and yards like tangled kite string hanging from a tree; bulwarks were riddled with jagged holes and planking was shredded; the gun deck was littered with gear tossed about in utter chaos; guns and slides were dismounted, tossed askew, or simply silent; and the wholesale butchery left the American flagship's gun deck strewn from bow to stern with dead, dying, and bleeding crewmen—four out of every five men fit for duty had been either killed or wounded.[104] Perry now faced the dismal prospect of surrender.

But as he glanced to larboard there floated the *Niagara*, almost abeam to windward between one and three cable lengths away, her carronades still cold and unfouled. Without hesitation, Perry made a fateful decision. An order was passed for the "DONT GIVE UP THE SHIP" flag to be lowered from the *Lawrence*'s main truck. Private Hosea Sergeant of the 17th U.S. Infantry was standing near the mainmast halyards when the order was given, and the one-time farmer and seaman from Maine (then Massachusetts) helped haul the flag down. This soldier with the unlikely moniker of Private Sergeant gingerly handed the symbolic blue banner to his commodore.[105] Command of the defenseless flagship was then turned over to Lieutenant Yarnall. While this was occurring the *Lawrence*'s first cutter was hauled up along the flagship's windward, or disengaged, side; the boat had been towed astern during the battle to prevent it from being blasted into shrapnel by British shot. Four men had jumped into the damaged cutter and were awaiting the commodore. Those officers and men still on their feet wanted to accompany Perry in order to continue the fight, but the commodore instructed them to remain on board to care for their savaged ship and tormented shipmates. Finished with the transfer of command, Perry, battle flag in hand, descended into the rowboat. Moments later the cutter's oarsmen were pulling furiously for the *Niagara*.[106]

Realizing the significance of the transfer—they were fairly certain it was Perry in the rowboat—the British shifted the focus of their fire to the little cutter. With great care John Chapman, a private in the 41st Regiment of Foot serving as a gunner on board the *Queen Charlotte*, aimed a 24-

pounder at the cutter and fired.[107] The shot just missed. Repeatedly during its entire perilous journey the cutter was inundated by the splashes of near misses, and the descending cascades of water soaked its frantically rowing crew. Miraculously, after passing through a storm of shot, Perry and his boat crew reached the *Niagara* unscathed.

Accounts vary as to exactly what transpired when Perry boarded the *Niagara*. One memoir relates that when the commodore climbed over the bulwark and descended the ladder onto *Niagara*'s gundeck, Jesse Elliott strode up to him and asked how the day was going![108] Considering that his flagship had been practically shot out from under him, he had suffered horrendous casualties, he was in danger of losing the battle, and his second largest ship—whose captain he was now staring in the eye—had not maneuvered to within carronade range during the past two hours, one can only imagine what was going through Perry's mind. Tersely the commodore replied, "badly."[109]

Regardless of what words were exchanged, Elliott shortly thereafter volunteered, for whatever reason, to board the *Lawrence*'s cutter and row back through the American line to hurry along the lagging schooners. Perry readily agreed to this astonishing proposal and Elliott departed immediately. Ordering his battle flag to be hoisted to the topmast of the *Niagara*, Perry instructed the tillermen to put the helm up.* The *Niagara* swung gracefully to starboard before steadying up on a course to pierce the British battle line just ahead of the *Detroit*.

Even though the British had pounded the *Lawrence* into submission, they had suffered terribly themselves. While injuries among the rankers were numerous, officer casualties were disproportionately high. Lieutenant Edward W. Buchan, commander of the *Lady Prevost*, took a nasty wound to his face, while Buchan's second in command, Lieutenant Frederick Rollette of the Provincial Marine, was badly contused on his left side and severely burned by a powder explosion. Lieutenant George Bignell, captain of the *General Hunter*, had been shot through the shoulder, and Bignell's first officer, Master's Mate Henry Gateshill, suffered a slight wound. Master's Mate John Campbell of the *Chippawa* was also slightly wounded.

Much of the damage inflicted upon the *Queen Charlotte* resulted from the *Caledonia*'s long guns. Most likely it was this little brig's heavy 24-pounder's that cut down the *Queen Charlotte*'s captain and acting-Marine

---

* The helm refers to either the ship's wheel or tiller. If the helm was put up it was turned into, or up wind.

officer early in the engagement:

> Captain [Robert] Finnis...was killed by a round shot...and
> the same ball carried off Lieutenant [James] Garden, a
> promising young officer of the Newfoundland Regiment,
> mingling the blood of the one and the brains of the other,
> on the bulwark, in one melancholy and undistinguishable
> mass.[110]

On board the British flagship, First Lieutenant John Garland was down with a mortal wound and the British commander himself had been slightly wounded when a small wood splinter penetrated his thigh. Barclay returned to the *Detroit's* gun deck and resumed command after being patched up by Surgeon George Young. But then, as the *Niagara* was approaching the British line, Barclay was struck again. The British commodore's second wound was severe, disabling his remaining good arm and forcing him below to the care of Surgeon Young. By the time the *Niagara* breached the British battle line the commander and first officer of each of the five largest British vessels had been either killed or wounded.[111] Due to attrition, the British ships were now commanded by junior officers; brave men, but with little or no experience handling ships in battle.

The menacing approach of the essentially undamaged *Niagara* convinced Lieutenant George Inglis, now the British flagship's senior officer, of the need to take remedial action. With many of his larboard guns out of action, Inglis knew that his only hope to stave off disaster was to wear ship and bring his undamaged starboard battery to bear.[112] *Detroit's* helm was put up as British sailors strained at the braces, attempting to haul the damaged yards around. Sluggishly the *Detroit* started to turn, her movements painfully slow due to her shot-riddled rigging and top hamper.

At this critical point in the battle, fate and Perry's extraordinary good fortune intervened to destroy any hope for victory that the British still retained. A number of options for trimming yards and sails were available to Lieutenant Inglis as he issued orders to wear the *Detroit* around. One theory holds that the British flagship's fore topsail yard was braced around until the sail was aback. The wind against the backed fore topsail would have been the quickest and easiest way to swing the *Detroit's* head around, but in order to complete her turn the *Detroit* would have had to maintain sufficient headway. Without that forward momentum the backed topsail's broad expanse of canvas would have acted as a brake, and the continued pressure against the backed topsail would have caused the flagship to begin gathering sternway.[113]

The Battle of Lake Erie

Meanwhile, as the *Detroit* was in the process of wearing ship, the *Queen Charlotte* was also maneuvering. Command of the *Queen Charlotte* devolved upon Royal Navy Lieutenant Thomas Stokoe after her captain and first lieutenant were felled, but a wood splinter cut down Stokoe just after the *Queen Charlotte* passed the *General Hunter*. Now under the command of Provincial Marine Lieutenant Robert Irvine, the *Queen Charlotte*, apparently preparing to wear around also, was easing up slightly to windward of her consort. Whether it was inexperience on the part of the junior British commanders, heavy damage suffered by the *Detroit* and *Queen Charlotte*, miscommunications, or a combination of factors is unknown, but in the confusion the *Detroit*, apparently in irons and now making sternway, "fell on board the *Queen Charlotte*."[114] The *Queen Charlotte*'s bowsprit gored its way through the *Detroit*'s tangled mizzen* rigging, skewering the British flagship. It is uncertain as to when the *Detroit*'s mizzen topmast and gaff fell, but had they remained in place prior to the collision, they came toppling down at this point, compounding the damage. And now, at the most crucial stage of the engagement, the two largest British ships were locked together and dangerously vulnerable.

Taking advantage of the British blunder, Perry sailed the *Niagara* through the British line. With three British ships to starboard and three to larboard, the commodore unleashed both of the *Niagara*'s double-shotted broadsides with devastating effect.

Though *in extremis*, the British ships still bared their teeth. Until this time the *Niagara* had incurred but little damage and few injuries, most accounts stating that before Perry boarded the brig she had suffered only two men wounded. That soon changed. As the *Niagara* eased toward and passed through Barclay's line "at half Pistol shot distance,"+ British guns that could be brought to bear concentrated on Perry's new flagship.[115] Iron, lead, and wood splinters cut down more than 20 Niagara crewmen in the next few minutes. Private John Reems of the 28th U.S. Infantry was struck either by musket balls or canister shot in the head and arm; the head wound sheared off a large piece of his skull just under his hairline.[116] Sergeant Sanford A. Mason of the 28th U.S. was hit in the left hand and arm by wood splinters, and Private George McManomy of the same regiment was

---

* On a ship with three or more masts, the third mast is called the mizzen.

+ Half pistol shot is an unspecified distance. Pistols of the period were notoriously inaccurate, but the maximum range of a pistol was about 50 to 75 yards, so half pistol shot would be approximately 25 to 35 yards.

peppered in his arms and legs by at least a half dozen wood splinters.[117]   A British cannonball smashed through the *Niagara*'s bulwark near gun number eight, driving a wood splinter deeply into the right leg of Ordinary Seaman John Bellamy, while Seaman James Lansford suffered a severe wound to his left leg; both crawled below to seek medical assistance.[118]   A British soldier, probably on the *Detroit*, put a musket ball into the right thigh of 1st U.S. Light Dragoon private Roswell Hall.[119]   Both Private Joshua Trapnell of the 17th U.S. Infantry and Private George Schofield of the 28th U.S. Infantry were severely wounded on the *Niagara*, and both were dead within a few days.[120]

Perry shortened sail as the *Niagara* forged through the British line, allowing the brig to lose headway so that she could continue to pound the already battered British ships. Adding to the destruction were the smaller American vessels that had initially lagged behind. Though somewhat scattered, a freshening breeze enabled the *Porcupine, Somers, Tigress*, and *Trippe* to haul within range and add their heavy long guns to the melee.

Observing the gunboats' approach and unwilling to expose their fragile timbers to the heavy American long guns, the commanders of the *Lady Prevost* and *Little Belt* spread additional sail and steered toward the head of the British line. The little sloop *Trippe*, initially last of the four American gunboats in line, put on a burst of speed and was the first of the trailing vessels to engage. Maneuvering near the stern of the *Detroit*, the *Trippe* raked the British flagship with her 24-pounder long gun. William Brady, a private with the 147th Pennsylvania Militia Regiment, not only served as a purser's steward on the *Trippe*, but he also volunteered to man that vessel's single heavy pivot gun as the shot and wadman. It was Brady's job to hand load powder and shot into the big 24-pounder's gaping maw. Being unfamiliar with artillery, Brady failed to appreciate the cannon's explosive effect and the muzzle blast from the first round ripped away half of his shirt and burned his arm. His lesson learned, Brady stepped clear for the second shot—at least he thought he was out of the way. The ill-starred militiaman actually stepped right into the path of a heavy wood tackle block, which smashed into his kneecap when the gun recoiled.[121]

Easing up astern of the *Trippe* was the *Somers*. Blazing away with her long 24-pounder, the gunboat hurled one of her 5½-inch diameter iron balls through the *Queen Charlotte*'s rudder.[122] Enemy gun crews replied to the scrappy little schooner's fire. A British cannonball plowed into the *Somers'* main boom, and one of the wood splinters that darted across the little vessel's deck speared the arm of Pennsylvania Militia Private Godfrey Bowman.[123]

The Battle of Lake Erie

The throaty, stentorian din emanating from the squadron's great guns was literally deafening. Private Harvey Harrington, a 27th U.S. Infantryman serving on the *Tigress*, was unable to hear anything because of the 32-pounder long gun's thunderous roar, and blast concussion squeezed a stream of blood from his ears.[124] Patrick FitzPatrick, the *Trippe*'s 55-year-old pilot, was likewise rendered deaf by that gunboat's 24-pounder long gun.[125] FitzPatrick was not the only crewman on board the squadron's lone sloop to experience hearing loss. The *Trippe*'s commander, Lieutenant Thomas Holdup, remembered that "a great proportion of my crew complained of deafness after the conflict," and Holdup himself did not fully recover his hearing until several days after the fight.[126]

The American crews had suffered terribly from British firepower, but the punishment inflicted upon the entangled *Detroit* and *Queen Charlotte* by *Niagara*'s carronades and the gunboats' long guns was even more deadly. Still, the unflinching officers and crewmen of Barclay's squadron refused to quit. With comrades falling on every side, the intrepid British and Canadians hacked feverishly at the snarled wreckage which triced the two ships together. Eventually the desperate effort paid off, the ravaged British ships separated and drifted apart. Thought was given to continuing the contest, but it was simply impossible. Conditions on the *Detroit* and *Queen Charlotte* were appalling: heavy casualties had been sustained, firepower was nullified, and spars and rigging were so badly damaged that the ships could barely maneuver. The *Detroit* was by far in the worst shape. Unrelenting broadsides of roundshot, grape, canister, and langrage from the ponderous 32-pounder carronades of the *Lawrence* and *Niagara* left the British flagship in an unmanageable state, with:

> …every Brace cut away, the Mizen [sic] Topmast and
> Gaff down, all the other Masts badly Wounded, not a Stay
> left forward, Hull shattered very much [and] a number of
> the Guns disabled...[127]

Lieutenant George Inglis had but little choice. He later reported conditions were such that:

> ...[the enemy's] Squadron, Raking [the *Detroit* and *Queen
> Charlotte*] ahead and astern, none of our own [vessels] in
> a situation to support us, I was under the painful necessity
> of answering the Enemy to say we had struck...[128]

The *Queen Charlotte* struck her colors first, soon followed by the *Detroit* and *General Hunter*. *Lady Prevost* emulated her larger consorts; the big schooner's commander, Lieutenant E. H. Buchan, was momentarily deranged from the pain of his ghastly face wound and the vessel's rudder had been badly mangled. The lesser damaged *Chippawa* and *Little Belt*, hoping to escape, loosed all sail and laid in a course for the Detroit River. Perry quickly ordered the *Scorpion* and *Trippe* to take up the chase. A lively pursuit ensued until the Americans closed the gap enough to toss a shot or two at the fleeing enemy, which convinced the last two survivors to strike; the three small cannons carried by the two British vessels were no match for the much larger caliber guns on the *Scorpion* and *Trippe*.

After the final shot echoed across the debris-strewn water, the two spent squadrons anchored about two miles to the north and east of West Sister Island. News of the victory needed to be conveyed to the American army. Grabbing his hat to use as a makeshift writing table, Perry hastily scribbled a note to William Henry Harrison. Written in pencil on the back of an old envelope, the commodore's message read:

> Dear General:
> We have met the enemy and they are ours:
> Two Ships, two Brigs, one
> Schooner & one Sloop.
> Yours with great respect and esteem
> O.H. Perry[129]

A short time later Perry scribed a more eloquent, though less dramatic letter to Secretary of the Navy William Jones:

> U.S. Brig *Niagara* off the Westward
> Sister Head of Lake Erie, Sepr. 10th 1813
> 4 p.m.
>
> Sir:
> It has pleased the almighty to give to the arms of the United States a signal victory over their enemies on this Lake. The British Squadron consisting of two Ships, two Brigs, one Schooner & one Sloop have this moment surrendered to the force under my command, after a sharp conflict.
> I have the honor to be
> Sir
> Very Respectfully
> Your Obdt. Servt.
> O.H. Perry[130]

The number of casualties suffered by both sides at the Battle of Lake Erie was relatively light when compared with losses incurred during most of the great battles of history, but the ratio of killed and wounded to numbers engaged was significant. American casualties reported by

The Battle of Lake Erie

Surgeon's Mate Usher Parsons totaled 27 killed and 96 wounded. Of the men whose wounds were listed as severe, at least eight proved mortal.[131] There were at least 13 additional Americans who were wounded or otherwise became casualties of the battle whose names did not, for one reason or another, appear on the casualty report.[132] These names added to the list would raise the number of American casualties to a minimum of 136.

The exact number of Americans who actually fought in the battle is uncertain. Many sources report a total of 532. However, the 532 figure incorporates only those crewmen who were paid prize money,* so this figure is not representative of the fleet aggregate. For various reasons a substantial number of names, at least 45, were somehow omitted from the prize list.[133] An example would be the 15 men who were killed in action whose relatives, presumably because none could not be found, were never paid prize money and thus they do not appear on Hambleton's prize list.

On 26 May 1814, while Purser Samuel Hambleton was in the process of compiling the prize list, he wrote a lengthy letter to Oliver Hazard Perry. In six separate instances throughout the course of that letter Hambleton specified that the number of men on board the American squadron was 596; although the crew of the *Ohio*, which missed the engagement, was later incorporated on the prize list, Hambleton did not include the *Ohio* sailors in the original tabulation that he sent to Perry.[134] The 596 figure is undoubtedly too high because Usher Parsons listed 116 men as being sick and unfit for duty just prior to the battle.[135] Many of these sick men struggled to perform their duty, but it is safe to assume that some were unable to fight. Deleting the 116 sick crewmen from the 596 enumerated by Hambleton would leave 480. Using an estimated 50% of the 116, possibly a high percentage, as being completely incapacitated during the engagement, and adding 30 of the 45 names that do not appear on Hambleton's list,+ then an estimate of Americans engaged in the battle

---

* When a warship or privateer was successful in battle it was common practice for that ship's government to purchase the captured enemy vessel for use by the navy. The money from that purchase—prize money—was divided among the crews that participated in the capture. Purser Samuel Hambleton was detailed by the Navy Department several months after the battle to compile a list of the U.S. Lake Erie squadron's crewmen in order that prize money could be distributed.

+ The 15 men killed in action whose names do not appear on the list were omitted presumably because they were not paid prize money. But Hambleton did not know when he first compiled the list that relatives of those men, who were legitimate heirs to the prize money, would not be found. They were entitled to prize money and as such they would have been included in Hambleton's original crew total of 596.

would be 568. Utilizing 568 as the actual number engaged and 136 as the total of killed and wounded, then the Americans suffered nearly 24% casualties.

Barclay reported British casualties as 41 killed and 96 wounded.[136] By combining Barclay's casualty list with the American prisoner of war returns, the British flotilla complement added up to approximately 560.[137] Data relating to British and Canadian sailors and soldiers who fought at the Battle of Lake Erie is not as complete as that for the American squadron, so the casualty figures reported by Barclay will have to be taken at face value. Using the numbers as recorded, British casualties amounted to 25% of the squadron total.

That same Friday evening, as the combined squadrons lay at anchor near West Sister Island, there was a pause in the hasty repair work as the American enlisted men who were killed in action were buried at sea. Exhausted American and British crewmen bowed their heads as Chaplain Thomas Breese read from the Episcopal burial service, after which the corpses splashed overboard, each enshrouded in his hammock or sewn in sail canvas and weighted down with a 32 pound cannonball. The reward for their supreme sacrifice was a small patch of mud 30 feet beneath Lake Erie's choppy surface. While a number of the British enlisted dead may have been interred in Lake Erie at the same time, many of the British soldiers and sailors who were killed in action, as per the custom, were heaved overboard during the engagement in order not to impede their comrades' efforts to fight their ships. Possibly some of the American dead experienced the same fate.[138]

At 0900 on Saturday morning the two squadrons, victorious American and captured British, catted their anchors and set sail for Put-in-Bay, where they anchored at meridian (1200). The following morning, Sunday, 12 September, the six officers who were killed in the engagement, three American and three British, were buried side by side on South Bass Island, the final act in the Battle of Lake Erie.[139]

Lake Erie was now undisputedly in American hands. Within days Perry began transporting the Harrison's army, recently relocated from Camp Seneca (Old Fort, Ohio) to Camp Portage (Port Clinton, Ohio) in anticipation of an American naval victory, to South Bass Island. Additional American units from Fort Meigs were also shifted to Put-in-Bay. By 23 September the American squadron, along with nearly 90 bateaux* which

---

* A bateaux was a large double-ended flat-bottomed rowboat used on the rivers and lakes of the northern United States and Canada.

had been built over the course of the summer on the Cuyahoga River at Cleveland, were hauling troops and supplies from South Bass Island to Middle Sister Island.[140]

With the Americans creeping ever closer to Amherstburg, British General Procter concluded that any attempt to defend his stronghold would be futile: the British flotilla had been eliminated, Fort Malden's supply warehouses were barren, and Procter's remaining forces were heavily outnumbered. On the very day that the Americans were consolidating at Middle Sister Island for the final push, a heavily laden British column slipped out of Fort Malden and tramped northward. To their rear, Fort Malden and the Amherstburg Navy Yard had been transformed into a raging conflagration. Accompanying the British was a disconsolate Tecumseh and his remaining loyal followers. The despondent Shawnee leader intuitively apprised one of his followers that, "We are going to follow the British, and I feel that I shall never return."[141]

Landing unopposed just below Amherstburg on the afternoon of 27 September, Harrison formed his army to pursue the retreating British. Procter's column, in the interim, turned eastward after passing through Sandwich and lumbered along the southern shore of Lake St. Clair to the mouth of the Thames River. Continuing up the Thames, Procter's demoralized troops plodded along the north bank, abandoning or destroying large quantities of supplies and equipment. Supplies were not the only items of importance being lost to the British. Disillusioned by the burning of Fort Malden and the disorderly retreat, Indians were disappearing into the forest by the hundreds.

Caught up in the chase, Commodore Perry was eager to take a more active role. Crossing the Thames River bar with the *Scorpion*, *Tigress*, and *Porcupine*, the only vessels on hand which could clear the bar, Perry sailed eastward in support of the army. It was not long thereafter that the impulsive Perry turned over command of the gunboats to Jesse Elliott, borrowed a horse, and attached himself to Harrison's staff as a volunteer aide.[142]

Meanwhile, the disjointed British army weltered in disorderly muddle. Plagued by constant rain, the bedraggled and discouraged redcoats trudged eastward through the soggy woods under dreary overcast skies. Of greater concern though was the insidious breakdown in the British system of command and control. Seemingly unable to focus on a plan of action, Procter more often than not absented himself from his main body of troops, preferring instead to ride ahead to reconnoiter the retreat route and ensure the safety of his family.

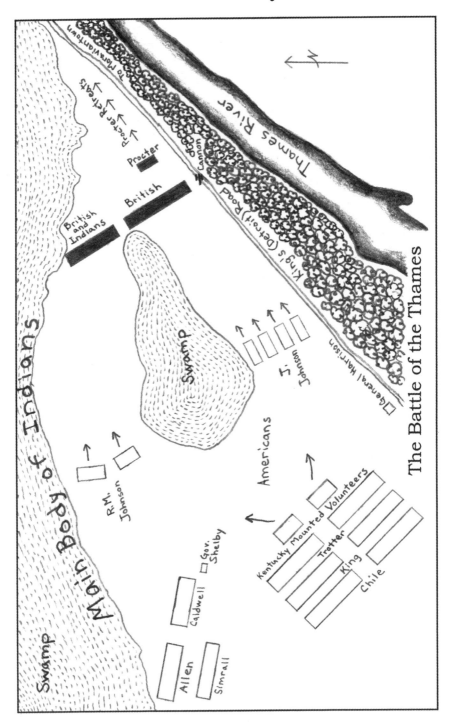

The Battle of the Thames

The Battle of Lake Erie

Even less happy than the British soldiers were Procter's Indian allies.* Tecumseh realized that the abandonment of Fort Malden marked the beginning of the end unless the invading Americans could be quickly defeated. In his defense, Procter faced no choice but to evacuate Fort Malden. The British flotilla had been captured, food supplies had dwindled to an alarming level, and there was no hope of resupply. Furthermore, British and Canadian troops at Amherstburg were expecting an imminent invasion by a vastly superior force that could easily surround their isolated post and cut off any possible withdrawal. If Procter had hesitated and waited until the last minute before retiring, Harrison could have landed farther to the east, raced northward, and cut off the British line of retreat, a course of action that the American general did consider.[143]

The British general was all too aware that Amherstburg was untenable. Still, Procter also knew that he had to placate his native allies. He managed to convince Tecumseh that a retreat was necessary, but to keep the Indians from totally deserting him the general assured the Indians that the army would turn and make a stand at the forks of the Thames River (present-day Chatham, Ontario). To seal his promise, Procter pledged to Tecumseh and his followers that, "we will mix our bones with [your] bones."[144] Nevertheless, as the retreating column reached the vicinity of the forks on 3 October, Procter was advised that the site was ill suited for a defensive battle, so the British column was ordered to continue its eastward march. Angered at this betrayal, Tecumseh, a band of his followers, and a small British rear-guard laid an ambush for the Americans at the forks. Warned of the trap by sympathizers, Harrison rushed forward two 6-pounder field pieces and opened fire, dispersing the enemy before they could muster any resistance. In utter despair, Tecumseh slogged after the retiring British column.

Procter finally turned to fight on 5 October 1813 just to the west of a Christian Indian village called Moraviantown (about one mile northeast of present-day Thamesville, Ontario).[145] Here the Thames River flows in a southwesterly direction, and the British situated their battle line on the north bank of the river in a lightly wooded area interspersed with small clearings. Facing southwest, the British regulars, in two lines, extended

---

* The generic designation of Indians tends to dehumanize the confusing and desperate plight of many Native American nations and individuals. Indians fought for both sides during the War of 1812, and for some tribes that divided loyalty resulted in civil war, but understandable self-interest led the majority to ally themselves with the British. Among nations that fell under the influence of Tecumseh and fought for the British in the Old Northwest were the Dakota, Delaware, Illinois, Iroquois, Kickapoo, Menominee, Miami, Ojibwa, Ottawa, Peoria, Piankashaw, Potawatomi, Sac and Fox, Shawnee, Winnebago, and Wyandot.

about 300 yards northwest of the river, bisecting the east-west running Detroit Road. The Detroit Road, in the center of which rested a 6-pounder field piece, anchored the British flank. Securing the flank was a mass of tangled and twisted brush that covered the 50 yards between the road and the steep bank of the river.

England's Indian allies prolonged the British line to the northwest until it entered a heavily wooded swamp that roughly aligned itself with the river approximately 650 yards north of the sluggish stream. Here the trees were thicker, with downed snags and slash interlaced to form a natural abatis,* providing a bulwark against mounted troops. Tecumseh extended his front westward for several hundred yards along the swamp's southern fringe. It was ground eminently suited to the Indians' style of warfare.

Slightly in advance of the British battle line, near the juncture of the British and Indian positions, lay another small swamp. This lesser marsh would require any attacking force to separate in order to avoid bogging down. The British line was roughly parabolic in shape and possessed several favorable defensive features. If properly fortified, the British and Indian emplacements could prove formidable indeed, and with the flanks securely anchored, the only offensive option for the Americans would be a headlong attack.

Harrison arrived opposite Procter's deployed formations early in the afternoon. Viewing the British preparations, the American commander was painfully aware that the cost of a frontal assault by his inexperienced militia infantry would be prohibitive—Harrison had detached the bulk of his regulars to garrison Sandwich, Fort Detroit, and Fort Covington, a temporary earthwork erected just south of burned Fort Malden. As Harrison was surveying the British line and pondering his dilemma, Colonel Richard M. Johnson—Congressman, war hawk, Kentucky colonel, and future Vice President of the United States—commanding a regiment of Kentucky mounted volunteers, rode up and impulsively requested permission to attack. Harrison demurred, knowing that a mounted attack against infantry in closed order was not tactically sound.

Being too distant from the British line to ascertain the enemy's dispositions, Harrison ordered Major Eleazor Wood to move forward and reconnoiter Procter's line. Upon his return, Wood informed Harrison that,

---

* Abatis are military engineering obstacles constructed by drilling holes in logs and threading sharpened stakes through the holes to form an "X" shaped pattern. Strategically placed on a battlefield, abatis are designed to direct or funnel an attacking line, and also to slow and hamper the attackers. Downed logs, brush, or debris, interwoven and piled in front of a battle line to serve as an obstacle to the enemy, are often simply referred to as abatis.

remarkably, the British were not aligned in closed order as anticipated, but loosely formed in open order, and no special effort was being made to strengthen or fortify their position.

It was Tecumseh who was responsible for the British and Indian tactics. Previously observing the red-coated regulars stiffly aligned in European style battle formation, the Indian leader perceived that fighting in wooded terrain required resourcefulness, not linear tactics.* Tecumseh recommended to Procter that the redcoats disperse behind trees and fight Indian style; he hoped that the British could stall Harrison's attack along its front while the Indians turned the American left flank. Procter deferred to the judgement of his guerilla-fighting expert. So, like the Indians, the British stood individually or in small knots behind trees, with larger groups in open order dotting the tiny clearings. For the British, it was a fatal error.

To Harrison, the British and Indian order of battle was a surprising and completely unexpected development, but the enemy's unusual alignment molded the American general's decision. Johnson's horsemen would spearhead the attack in the hope that an assault by mounted troops would furnish tactical surprise and clinch a victory. Marshalling about 950 riders, Richard Johnson divided his 12 companies evenly into two battalions. He elected to send one battalion, commanded by his elder brother, Lieutenant Colonel James Johnson, against the British regulars. Having no family, unlike his brother James, Richard Johnson reserved the more hazardous task for himself: assaulting the unpredictably dangerous Indians.

An unsettled hush cloaked the opposing lines as both sides girded for the imminent clash. Some of the mounted troops, waiting nervously astride skittish horses, undoubtedly recalled their passage through Frenchtown about ten days earlier. On that somber day the heartsick Kentuckians gathered and buried the bleached bones of their fellow Bluegrass soldiers, left scattered where they fell the previous January following the River Raisin debacle. That grisly memory was bitterly fresh in their minds.

Finally, between 1500 and 1600, a dismounted line of American skirmishers darted agilely across the field in measured leaps. As the first

---

* Linear tactics, or line of battle, as practiced by European armies called for large formations of soldiers to stand shoulder to shoulder in two or more lines. Such tactics were employed to maximize efficiency, or inefficiency, of the flintlock musket, the standard infantry weapon of the day. The single-shot, muzzle-loading, smoothbore musket was inaccurate at best and possessed an effective range of less than 100 yards. Infantry tactics dictated tight battle formations with opposing lines firing at close range; the objective was to hurl a wall of lead from massed ranks of infantry muskets. Also, a cohesive battle line of several hundred or several thousand disciplined soldiers advancing with leveled bayonets offered an incredibly intimidating, demoralizing, and terrorizing specter.

sharp cracks of musketry echoed through the autumn foliage, a bellowed command to charge propelled a thundering mass of hooves across the narrow plain. Amidst the galloping horsemen a single resonant shout pierced the sonorous pounding of shod horses: "Remember the Raisin!" The simple yet emotional battle cry spread like wildfire, fomenting a deep and abiding undercurrent of violence among the embittered horse soldiers.

In double line, James Johnson's four columns of black-frocked mounted riflemen swarmed toward the British position, their right flank approximately 50 yards north of the narrow wilderness road. Suddenly, a spattering of musketry spewed from the woods to their front, a hurried and seemingly half-hearted volley that barely disrupted the orderly charge. Moments later the swift-riding American horsemen reached the line of widely spaced British troops. Scattered in open order, the British soldiers, mostly regulars from the 41st Regiment of Foot, were not properly deployed to check the mounted onslaught. The Kentuckians slashed through their ranks, sweeping past the double British line. Gaining the enemy rear, James Johnson's men wheeled their horses and began picking off the confused redcoats from behind. Defeated and dispirited, the British regulars broke and ran. Within minutes the Kentucky horse battalion was harvesting a bumper crop of dejected British prisoners. Private Shadrach Byfield of the 41st Foot succinctly described the feeble British resistance:

> After exchanging a few shots, our men gave way. I was in
> the act of retreating when one of our sergeants exclaimed,
> 'For God's sake, men, stand and fight.' I stood by him
> and fired one shot, but the line was broken and the men
> were retreating.[146]

The British left had crumpled, but on the opposite flank the fighting was more desperate. Kentuckians and Indians, diametrically opposed factions who traditionally harbored an implacable and remorseless hatred for the other, amply manifested their rancor by the ferocity with which they battled one another. Richard Johnson's battalion had formed in double column for the assault. Preceding the main attack, however, was a small band of 20 volunteers referred to as the forlorn hope. The premise behind the forlorn hope was that the first enemy volley would be squandered on this initial foray, thereby allowing the main force to assail a line of empty weapons.

It was a sound, if somewhat gruesome, philosophy. When the small group of riders raced forward a ragged line of muzzle flashes illuminated the gloomy treeline to their front. Horses and men tumbled to the earth, 15 of the 20 stalwart Kentuckians were either killed or wounded. The volley's

William Henry Harrison

Henry Procter

echo was still reverberating through the woods when the two columns of shrieking horsemen spurred toward the treeline and struck Tecumseh's line, where frantic efforts to reload smoking muskets attested to the forlorn hope's success.

Ominously for Richard Johnson's battalion, the Indian position possessed inherently stronger defensive merits than that of the British regulars. The swampy ground and thick natural abatis prevented the Kentuckians from using their horses to advantage; they were unable to breach the Indian barricade. As the firing became general Johnson realized his mounts were proving a hindrance, so he ordered his men to dismount and fight on foot. Johnson's troops found themselves hard pressed by the fierce warriors, infantry would have to be rushed forward to bolster the American line.

The Americans had charged into a hornet's nest, but the Indians were also experiencing difficulties. An immediate threat had been posed to Tecumseh's left, or southern flank, by the retreat of Procter's regulars. Pressed on that quarter by James Johnson's jubilant men, who had wheeled their horses to the north after the British line has disintegrated, the warriors fought valiantly while giving ground gradually. On the far right, however, where they were not yet engaged, the Indians observed a lack of activity by Harrison's militia infantry, who were initially held in reserve while the mounted regiment attacked. Recognizing a potential weakness in the American troop dispositions, Tecumseh's warriors seized the opportunity and assumed the offensive. Striking the American regiments near the juncture of two militia brigades, the fearsome tribesmen forged a wedge between the two columns and compelled the inexperienced militiamen on Harrison's left front to give ground.

Harrison, with help from Kentucky Governor Isaac Shelby and Oliver Hazard Perry, quickly rallied the wavering foot soldiers and braced the American line with a fresh Kentucky militia regiment. The Americans soon shunted in even more infantry reinforcements, turning the tide for Harrison's army. Faced with conventional tactics and fresh troops, Tecumseh's fighting men could not sustain the initial ardor of their attack. Pressured to retire, the warriors resumed their original positions and continued to resist the American thrust.

Near the Indians left flank, Richard Johnson had suffered four distinct wounds, but he refused evacuation from the field. One of the few men still mounted, Johnson was struggling to stay erect on his crippled steed—the horse had been struck seven times—when a lone Indian suddenly confronted him. Darting from the treeline, the dauntless warrior raised his musket and fired, striking Johnson on his hand and inflicting the colonel's fifth wound. Johnson reeled, somehow maintaining his seat in the saddle. The relentless Indian then raised a tomahawk and rushed toward the swaying colonel. Struggling desperately, Johnson somehow managed to draw his pistol, loaded with buck and ball.* Johnson shot the Indian in the chest only seconds before he was able to swing his deadly hatchet.

Many veterans of the battle later declared that Johnson's victim was none other than Tecumseh. The colonel himself neither confirmed nor denied that assertion. Considering his debilitated condition and his evacuation from the field immediately afterwards, it is entirely plausible that Johnson never knew his assailant's identity. Regardless of whether or not it was Tecumseh who Johnson had shot, the great Shawnee leader was killed about this time, and the death of their patriarch effectively snuffed out the Indian flame. Within minutes the leaderless tribesmen melted into the woods, and for all intents and purposes, as far as the Old Northwest was concerned, the Indians faded into the history books.

The human cost at the Thames was amazingly light considering the nature of the combatants and the style of fighting. Harrison reported a total of seven killed and 22 wounded; so rapid was the British collapse that James Johnson's columns on the American right flank suffered only three men wounded. British casualties were 12 killed and 22 wounded; however, the bulk of the Procter's regulars were snared as prisoners, with only about 50 of the roughly 500 redcoats managing to escape into the woods. Indian losses were more difficult to ascertain. Harrison counted 33 dead warriors on the field, but an unknown number of dead and wounded Indians were carried from the field by their comrades.

The Battle of the Thames was another decisive American victory. Procter's forces had been routed and the disheartened remnants were in full retreat. Although the British regrouped at Burlington, Governor General Sir George Prevost opted not to conduct further operations in the Western District of Upper Canada due to limited resources and continued American pressure in the Niagara and St. Lawrence River regions. As for Great Britain's allies, Tecumseh was dead, his confederacy had been destroyed, and the grief-stricken warriors had scattered, no longer a force with which to be reckoned. So convincing was their defeat that several of the tribes

---

* Buck and ball, often used in smoothbore muskets and pistols, was a deadly round that comprised a normal sized ball plus three double-ought buckshot. If the gun was .69 caliber (caliber is diameter in inches), then the round would have been composed of a ball .63 of an inch in diameter—it was necessary for the ball to be slightly smaller than the caliber of the weapon—and three .32 caliber buckshot.

signed a formal armistice agreement with Harrison on 16 October.

Harrison's victory was complete. Choosing not to pursue his conquered enemy, the general withdrew the American army to the Detroit River. The campaign's objectives had been fulfilled: control of Lake Erie had been secured, and Fort Detroit and the Detroit River corridor were firmly in the grasp of United States forces. With the enemy defeated and winter rapidly approaching there was no further need to maintain a large army in the region. The majority of the American regulars, except for those detached to garrison the various fortifications, were transferred to the Niagara River area over the next few weeks for deployment during future operations. Harrison's Kentucky militia regiments were discharged and sent home.

Despite his overwhelming success in leading American ground forces to victory in the Northwest Territory, William Henry Harrison was not selected for another command. In the months following the battle he was feted as a hero by the American populace, but the general's future was relegated to the hands of Washington's political power brokers, where his newfound popularity made him a threat. Undermined by political enemies and intolerant of those who fostered such divisiveness, Harrison submitted his resignation from the army on 11 May 1814. He spent the rest of the war in semi-retirement at his home in North Bend, Ohio, just west of Cincinnati.

Perry returned to Erie along with most of his squadron and the British Navy commander. In the weeks following the battle a rapport developed between the opposing naval leaders. It was through Perry's intercession with the Navy Department that a quick and compassionate pardon was arranged for Barclay so that he could return home to recover from his debilitating wounds. One year minus a day following the battle, Barclay was subjected to a court-martial for the loss of the British squadron. After testimony was heard, Barclay was acquitted of all charges, the court ruling:

> That the judgement and Gallantry of Captain Barclay in
> taking his squadron into Action and during the Contest
> were highly conspicuous and entitled him to the highest
> Praise and that the whole of the Officers and Men of His
> Majesty's late Squadron conducted themselves in the most
> gallant Manner...[147]

Barclay himself aptly summed up British efforts two days after the engagement when he wrote, "...the honour of his Majesty's flag has not been tarnished..."[148] And it was not.

Perry followed through with his 10 August request for transfer. On 25 October, after transporting Harrison's regulars to the eastern end of the lake, Perry resigned his command while at Buffalo and turned over the Lake Erie squadron to Elliott.[149] From there he returned to Rhode Island to resume his duties with the gunboat flotilla at Newport until a posting more commensurate with his new status could be found—his victory prompted Perry's immediate promotion to captain, to date from 10 September 1813.

Jesse Elliott remained in command of the Lake Erie squadron through the winter of 1813, but in April of 1814 he was replaced by Captain Arthur Sinclair, transferred to Lake Ontario, and assigned as the commanding officer of the 20-gun brig *Sylph*. In November of 1814 Elliott was given command of the 22-gun sloop-of-war *Ontario*, then fitting out at Baltimore, but "his hopes of gathering fresh laurels upon the ocean were defeated by the peace of 1815."[150]

If any one faction can be said to have lost the War of 1812 it would have to be the Indians. Tecumseh was dead, as was any hope the Indians might have retained for restoring the Northwest Territory to Native American control. But Tecumseh's followers were not the only Indians to suffer, the fortunes of all tribes living east of the Mississippi River sustained a devastating and irreversible blow. Great Britain virtually abandoned their allies, particularly at the peace talks, leaving Native Americans without an advocate on the world stage. The death of Tecumseh and the military defeat at the Thames proved to be a ruinous tumble over a waterfall on the Indian river of decline; a river that flowed inexorably westward.

Lake Erie quickly became a backwater of the war after the American victories on Lake Erie and at the Thames River. For the remainder of the war the British were unable to mount a serious threat against United States forces west of the Niagara region. With the exception of some periodic skirmishing and a failed American attempt to retake Fort Michilimackinac during the summer of 1814, the War of 1812 in the Old Northwest was over.

AFTERWORD

The decisive United States naval victory on Lake Erie on 10 September 1813 spawned several significant developments that either affected the outcome of the War of 1812 or directly influenced America's ability to continue the struggle. Oliver Hazard Perry's victory crushed British naval strength on Lake Erie, secured control of the lake, and enabled Harrison's troops to be transported simply and efficiently to the Canadian mainland. The outnumbered and demoralized British and Indian force was then handily defeated at the Thames River. These tandem victories provided the United States peace commissioners at Ghent, Belgium with their only major bargaining chip during the next eight crucial months of negotiations. Valuable time had been gained for the American peace emissaries and British contempt for American military prowess was tempered until further triumphs during the summer of 1814 solidified their position.

Moreover, the victory was achieved at a crucial point in the war. The United States had suffered a demoralizing string of outright defeats or tactical stalemates on land during the first 15 months of the war, and an initial spate of victories at sea had been reversed when the British Admiralty deployed larger and better armed warships to meet the American naval threat. Perry's victory served as an important morale booster for the country, providing the necessary resolve to continue the struggle.

The success of American military efforts in the Old Northwest and their subsequent impacts was due in no small part to Oliver Hazard Perry. With the exception of his tenure on Lake Erie, Perry's life and naval career were anything but spectacular. But as a result of this three-hour battle, Perry will always be remembered by history as the hero of Lake Erie, and his stirring, unforgettable words "We have met the enemy and they are ours," will endure as a mainstay of American naval lore.

However, the real story of the Battle of Lake Erie belongs to the men who comprised the haggard crews of Perry's makeshift fleet of warships. Tremendous credit belongs to those little remembered sailors, soldiers, and Marines who fought, suffered, and in many cases, died for their country. Those that survived would carry with them the pain and horror of that battle for the remainder of their lives. With little recognition and only their prize money to comfort them, they soon faded into obscurity. Yet they were the backbone of a frontier battle that materially affected the outcome of the War of 1812, and they helped preserve forever the five states of the Old Northwest as an integral part of the United States of America.

Appendix A

American Squadron Armament - 10 September 1813

Vessel	Guns (total)	Carronades	Long Guns	Metal (lb. total)	Broadside (lb.)
Lawrence	20	18 (32's)	2 (12's)	600	300
Niagara	20	18 (32's)	2 (12's)	600	300
Caledonia	3	1 (32 on pivot)	2 (24's on pivots)	80	80
Ariel	4	0	4 (12's, 2 on pivots)	48	36
Scorpion	2	1 (32 on pivot)	1 (32 on pivot)	64	64
Somers	2	1 (32 on pivot)	1 (24 on pivot)	56	56
Porcupine	1	0	1 (32 on pivot)	32	32
Tigress	1	0	1 (32 on pivot)	32	32
Trippe	1	0	1 (24 on pivot)	24	24
	54	39	15	1,536	924

Squadron Armament

British Squadron Armament - 10 September 1813

Vessel	Guns (total)	Carronades	Long Guns	Metal (lb. total)	Broadside (lb.)
Detroit	19	1 (24) 1 (18)	2 (24's) 1 (18 on pivot) 6 (12's) 8 (9's)	252	138
Queen Charlotte	17	14 (24's)	3 (12's, 1 on pivot)	372	192
Lady Prevost	13	10 (12's)	3 (9's, 1 on pivot)	147	78
General Hunter	10	2 (12's)	2 (6's) 4 (4's) 2 (2's)	56	28
Little Belt	3	0	1 (9 on pivot) 2 (6's)	21	15
Chippewa	1	0	1 (9 on pivot)	9	9
	63	28	35	857	460

Appendix B

Roll of Honor

BARCLAY, Robert Heriot: Commander, Royal Navy, *Detroit*. Because of his defeat on Lake Erie the Royal Navy subjected Barclay to an obligatory court-martial; he was exonerated of all blame. On 11 August 1814, during his convalescent leave, Barclay married Agnes Cossar and they moved to Saxe-Cobourg Place in Edinburgh, Scotland. There the Barclays raised a family of eight children. Barclay's health had been broken as a result of his wounds and the defeat reduced his stock with the Royal Navy. Not promoted to post captain until 1824, the only command the Royal Navy would give to the invalid officer was the *Infernal*, a tiny bomb vessel, so he opted to retire from the navy shortly thereafter. Barclay died in Edinburgh on 8 May 1837.

BELLAMY, John: Ordinary Seaman, U.S. Navy, *Niagara*. Bellamy joined the U.S. Navy in June of 1812 and served on Gunboat Number 81 before being shipped to the lakes in 1813. Some years after the battle his right leg developed an ulcer, possibly a result of his wound, and complications from the injury reportedly prevented him from holding a job. He submitted a pension application, but no record of a pension being issued could be found. Bellamy was living in Erie, Pennsylvania in 1830.

BIGNELL, George: Lieutenant, Royal Navy, *General Hunter*. During the War of 1812, Bignell was loaned from the *Dover*, then lying at Quebec, to command the *General Hunter* on Lake Erie (details concerning the *Dover* are sketchy; most likely it was a Franco-Italian 32-gun ship built at Bellona in 1806, captured by the British in 1811, and converted to a troopship). According to Barclay, Bignell "Displayed the greatest intrepidity" during the battle. Bignell had been promoted to lieutenant in 1801 and to commander on 19 September 1815.

BOWMAN, Godfrey: Private, 147th Regiment of Pennsylvania Militia, *Somers*. Bowman was granted a three-quarter's disability pension of $6.00 per month commencing 15 October 1825 (a full-disability pension at this time was $8.00 per month, and pensions were issued in fractions, such as one-half, two-thirds, etc.; it appears that the amount allowed for any particular pension was purely arbitrary). By 1820 he had moved from Kingston Township in Luzerne County, Pennsylvania to Brookfield in Tioga County, where he still resided in 1838.

BRADY, William: Private, 147th Regiment of Pennsylvania Militia, *Trippe*. A cabinet-maker by trade, Brady lived in Aaronsburg, Pennsylvania before the war. In 1846 he was elected the assistant sergeant-at-arms of the Pennsylvania Senate, and in 1848 he was awarded a $10.00 per month pension from the state. Brady died at Harrisburg on 4 April 1864.

BREESE, Thomas: Chaplain, U.S. Navy, *Lawrence*. Breese was not a true man of the cloth (the title of chaplain in the U.S. Navy was for the most part honorary; the incumbent usually served as an aide to the captain and as a teacher to the midshipmen). After working in a mercantile house in New York before the war, he returned to

Roll of Honor

Newport, Rhode Island—his hometown—to care for his widowed mother. Becoming weary of that chore, he applied to O. H. Perry at the Newport Naval Station for an appointment and Perry accepted Breese as his private secretary. Breese later served as chaplain under Captain Arthur Sinclair during the upper lakes campaign in 1814. Remaining in the navy after the war, Breese achieved the rank of purser and he was assigned to several ships and shore stations during his 35-year career. On 25 May 1825 Breese married Lucy Maria Randolph at Newport, and they raised a family of four sons and three daughters. The Breese family was living in Cambridge, Massachusetts, where Breese was assigned to the Charlestown Navy Yard, when he died of an unspecified disease on 11 October 1846.

BREVOORT, Henry B.: Captain, 2nd U.S. Infantry Regiment, *Niagara*. Brevoort was promoted to major in 1814 before being discharged when the war ended in 1815. He was appointed the United States Indian Agent at Green Bay, Wisconsin Territory in 1822. Brevoort was originally from New York, but he lived in the Detroit River region for most of his life. He died at Detroit in 1856.

BROOKS, John: Lieutenant, U.S. Marine Corps, *Lawrence*. Killed in action on 10 September 1813, he was buried on South Bass Island. The USS *Brooks* (DD 232) was named in honor of the fallen Marine lieutenant.

BROWN, Noah: Master Shipwright, Civilian Contractor. Born in northern New York in 1770, Brown and his three brothers survived a period of captivity after Indians killed their father. Later he lived in Stamford, New York. Trained as a carpenter, Brown worked at that trade in New York City until 1804, when he went into the shipbuilding business with his brother Adam. Over the next several years the Brown brothers built vessels for both the private sector and for the U.S. Navy. Following his work on Lake Erie, Brown returned to New York and built the U.S. Sloop-of-War *Peacock*. In 1814 he went to Lake Champlain, where he built the *Saratoga*, Commodore Thomas Macdonough's flagship, and he also worked on several of the other Lake Champlain vessels. Brown continued in the shipbuilding profession after the war. He was still living in New York City in 1833, but little is known of his activities after that time.

BUCHAN, Edward: Lieutenant, Royal Navy, *Lady Prevost*. In his official report, Barclay reported that Buchan "Behaved most nobly and did everything that a brave and experienced officer could do."

BUNNELL, David: Seaman, U.S. Navy, *Niagara*. Promoted to Purser's Steward on 23 March 1814, Bunnell became a prisoner of war during the late summer of 1814 when the *Scorpion* and *Tigress*—Bunnell was attached to the former vessel—were captured on Lake Huron. He subsequently spent time in Dartmoor prison in England, but was back in Boston by late 1815. In 1831 Bunnell published his memoirs in a work entitled, *Travels and Adventures of David C. Bunnell*.

BURDEEN, John: Seaman, U.S. Navy, *Lawrence*. A seaman by occupation before and after the war, Burdeen was a native of Ireland. On 22 May 1814, Captain Arthur Sinclair, then the senior naval officer on Lake Erie, certified that Burdeen had lost the use of his right leg as a result of the wound he suffered on 10 September 1813. On 25 June 1814, a surgeon in Washington, D.C. examined Burdeen's leg and recorded that "...the wound of his foot is still open..." As a result, Burdeen was issued a pension of $6.00 per month retroactive to

The Battle of Lake Erie

10 September 1813. Burdeen, who was married with an unknown number of children, died in a Massachusetts hospital on 24 June 1830.

BYFIELD, Shadrach: Private, 41st Regiment of Foot, British Army. Byfield was born at Wooley, near Bradford, in the county of Wilts on 16 September 1789. He enlisted in the army in 1807 and two years later his regiment, the 41st Foot, was shipped to North America. Byfield fought at Fort Detroit, the River Raisin, Fort Meigs, and Fort Stephenson; he was one of the few lucky soldiers of the 41st Foot to escape capture at the Thames. He saw action at Fort Niagara on 19 December 1813, Lundy's Lane on 25 July 1814, and three weeks later, on 13 August 1814, he was severely wounded in the left arm during a British raid north of Black Rock. Mortification soon set in and Byfield's arm had to be amputated. Byfield returned to England in December of 1814, where he was awarded a 9 pence per day pension, an amount that was eventually increased by 3 pence per day. For the next 20 years the one-armed Byfield supported his family working for a clothier in Bradford.

CAMPBELL, John: Master's Mate, Royal Navy, *Chippawa*. Wounded in action, 10 September 1813.

CHAPMAN, John: Private, 41st Regiment of Foot, *Queen Charlotte*. After the battle Chapman, along with other British prisoners, was incarcerated at Chillicothe, Ohio. Released on 20 October 1814, he took up residence in Hudson, Ohio, where he worked as a stone mason and lived for the rest of his life. Chapman filed naturalization papers and became a U.S. citizen in 1843. He died in 1866 and is buried in Twinsburg, Ohio.

CHAUNCEY, Isaac: Captain, U.S. Navy. Even though he was not within 400 miles of the Battle of Lake Erie, Chauncey received $12,000 in prize money since he was the overall commander of Great Lakes naval operations. After the war he was given command of a squadron of ships in the Mediterranean. Returning to the U.S. in 1818, Chauncey was appointed to the post of navy commissioner in Washington. He commanded the Brooklyn Navy Yard for a period of time, but was reappointed navy commissioner in 1833. Chauncey died in Washington, D.C. on 27 January 1840.

CHRISTIE, David: Private, U.S. Marine Corps, *Lawrence*. Complications from his wound caused Christie to be discharged from the Marine Corps on 1 January 1816. As of that date he received a half-disability pension of $4.00 per month. His wound was still suppurating in 1818. After his discharge he lived in Carlisle, Pennsylvania, but he had moved to West Ovington, New York by 1823. By 1841 he had relocated to Little Rock, Arkansas, where he was indigent except for his $4.00 per month pension. Christie left no family when he died in Little Rock on 30 October 1847.

CLARK, John: Midshipman, U.S. Navy, *Scorpion*. Killed in action on 10 September 1813, he was buried on South Bass Island. A U.S. Navy destroyer (DD 361) was named to commemorate Clark's service.

CLAXTON, Thomas: Midshipman, U.S. Navy, *Lawrence*. Died on 7 October 1813 due to complications from wounds incurred on 10 September 1813. Two U.S. Navy destroyers (DD 140 and DD 571) were named after Claxton.

Roll of Honor

CORNELL, George: Carpenter's Mate, U.S. Navy, *Lawrence*. Cornell was disabled for some time after the battle, but he remained with the squadron despite the severity of his wound. His pension file relates that he was taken prisoner on 20 August 1814, probably during the campaign on the upper lakes. He returned home to Newport, Rhode Island after the war and married Maria Rodman on 8 November 1815. They lived at the corner of Elm and Cross streets, later moving to 6 Mann Avenue. In 1826 a surgeon certified that Cornell:

> ...has been afflicted a long time, with a very uncommon dizziness, in his head; so as to affect his eye sight, & produce, a paralytic affliction of his mouth, & left eye; & so severe as to disqualify him for any business. That he has now, an extreme inflammation in his Head, with a discharge of ulcerous matter from his left Ear; so severe as to confine him to his bed....

Cornell reported he had been subject to such complications since the day of his wound. As a result, he was awarded a navy pension on 23 December 1826. George Cornell died at Newport on 26 May 1858.

CROSBY, Ebenezer: Master Shipwright, Civilian Contractor. Little is known about Crosby. When he entered into the contract to assist Daniel Dobbins in 1813 he was a resident of Niagara County, New York. He performed the actual on-sight supervision of ship construction at Erie until Noah Brown arrived in March. Nothing could be found concerning Crosby after June of 1813.

DOBBINS, Daniel: Sailing Master, U.S. Navy, *Ohio*. Dobbins was born near Lewistown, Pennsylvania on 5 July 1776. He married Mary West near Canonsburg, Pennsylvania on 1 April 1800, and they raised a family of eight children. On 1 July 1796 he visited Erie for the first time, making the lakeshore town his home shortly thereafter; in 1816 he built a home at the northeast corner of 3rd and State Streets. From 1800 through 1812 Dobbins was engaged on various merchant vessels on the Great Lakes. Dobbins remained with the Lake Erie squadron throughout the war and stayed in the U.S. Navy until resigning in 1826. He built piers in Ashtabula, Ohio until he was appointed to the Revenue Cutter Service (predecessor of the U.S. Coast Guard) in 1829. After serving intermittently as commanding officer of the cutters *Rush* and *Erie*, he retired in 1849 at age 73. Dobbins died at Erie on 29 February 1856.

EASTERBROOK, Jeremiah: Ordinary Seaman, U.S. Navy, *Lawrence*. Easterbrook was disabled as a result of his wound. In 1814 a surgeon at the Washington Navy Yard declared that Easterbrook had "lost the use of his leg, in consequence of the contraction of his knee joint...he will remain lame for life, his leg being of no use to him...." On 22 May 1814 he was issued a $5.00 per month disability pension payable at Boston.

ELLIOTT, Jesse Duncan: Master Commandant, U.S. Navy, *Niagara*. Elliott served as the senior officer on Lake Erie for a time after Perry departed in October 1813, but he was eventually replaced and transferred to Lake Ontario. In November of 1814 he was given command of the sloop-of-war *Ontario* and in 1815 sailed to the Mediterranean in a squadron under Stephen Decatur. Prior to sailing to Europe, Elliott requested a court-of-inquiry to review his actions on Lake Erie. Held in New York in April of 1815, the court ruled that any comments detrimental to Elliott's role in the battle were "malicious and unfounded." In 1818, having returned from the Mediterranean, Elliott discovered that Perry was writing letters criticizing his conduct on Lake Erie. Elliott challenged Perry to a duel, but the latter instead filed formal court-martial charges. Not wishing to reopen old wounds, the Secretary of the Navy and the President of the United States dealt with the matter unofficially. Elliott was promoted to captain in 1818 and held various commands over the next 27 years. In 1840 he was charged with misconduct and sentenced to a four-year suspension in service; President John Tyler remitted the last year of his sentence and Elliott was returned to duty in 1844. Elliott died on 18 December 1845.

FINNIS, John: Lieutenant, Royal Navy, *Queen Charlotte*. Finnis was transferred to Lake Erie in May of 1813, where he was given command of the *Queen Charlotte*. Finnis was killed in action on 10 September 1813 and he was buried on South Bass Island.

FITZPATRICK, Patrick: Pilot, U.S. Navy, *Trippe*. Despite his continuing deafness as a result of the battle, FitzPatrick worked as a laborer for as long as he was physically able. At some point he moved to Detroit, Michigan, where he applied for a disability pension; on 22 May 1828 the pension request was granted. FitzPatrick died at Detroit in 1831.

FORREST, Dulaney: Midshipman, U.S. Navy, *Lawrence*. A native of the District of Columbia, Forrest was warranted a midshipman in the U.S. Navy on 18 May 1809. He was attached to the U.S. Frigate *Constitution* when Old Ironsides defeated H.M. Frigate *Java* on 29 December 1812. In April of 1813 he was transferred to Lake Ontario, and in July of that year he was sent to Lake Erie. Forrest was appointed an acting-lieutenant by Perry and in that role he served as the second lieutenant of the *Lawrence* during the battle. After the engagement he was accorded the honor of bearing Perry's official report along with the captured British battle flags to Washington. He was commissioned a lieutenant on 9 December 1814 and he served under Perry on board the U.S. Frigate *Java* after the war. Forrest's promising naval career was cut short when he died of fever on board the USS Decoy on 1 October 1825. During World War II a U.S. Navy destroyer (DD-461) was named after him.

GARWOOD, Samuel: Private, U.S. Marine Corps, *Lawrence*. Garwood remained in the hospital for several weeks after the battle with blood draining from his ears. On 4 October 1813, upon his release at Erie, he deserted from the Marines. Years later a doctor certified that complications from his injury were causing bouts of temporary insanity, and despite his desertion, the government awarded Garwood a full disability pension of $8.00 per month. Garwood moved several times over the years, and in 1850 he was living in Luzerne Township, Fayette County, Pennsylvania.

GARDEN, James: Lieutenant, Royal Newfoundland Regiment, *Queen Charlotte*. Killed in action on 10 September 1813, he was buried on South Bass Island.

GARLAND, John: Lieutenant, Royal Navy, *Detroit*. Killed in action on 10 September 1813, he was buried on South Bass Island.

GATESHILL, Henry: Master's Mate, Royal Navy, *General Hunter*. Wounded in action, 10 September 1813.

HALL, Roswell: Private, 1st U.S. Light Dragoons, *Niagara*. Hall remained with the Lake Erie squadron until being discharged on 15 March 1815. In 1819 a surgeon verified that, as a result of his wound, Hall's right leg was somewhat shortened and wasted; he was issued a two-thirds disability pension of $5.00 per month on 22 January 1820. On 7 May 1832 a physician decreed that the musket ball was still lodged in Hall's thigh and that his leg condition rated a total disability; it is not known if his pension amount was increased. Hall lived in both Buffalo and Attica, New York after the war, but he had moved to Lenawee County, Michigan by May of 1837.

HAMBLETON, Samuel: Purser, U.S. Navy, *Lawrence*. A native of Talbot County, Maryland, Hambleton was born in 1777. He worked as a merchant in Georgetown, D.C. for some years before becoming a clerk in the Navy Department. This led to his appointment as a purser in the U.S. Navy on 6 December 1806. Hambleton was assigned to the New Orleans station for 4½ years before returning to Washington in July of 1811. In July of 1812 he was ordered to the Newport Naval Station, where he began his association with Perry. After the battle he continued to suffer from the effects of his shoulder injury until, in mid-November, a piece of bone suppurated from the still open wound. On 17 February 1814, Hambleton was ordered back to Washington, where he served as prize agent for the Lake Erie squadron. Hambleton remained in the navy for a number of years before retiring to the life of a gentleman farmer. In 1834 a navy surgeon examined Hambleton and reported that he found "evidence of an extensive wound of the left shoulder, with fracture & exfoliation of the bone, by which the motions of the joint, & of the general power of the arm have been materially impaired." Hambleton died at "Perry's Cabin," his residence near St. Michael's, Maryland, on 17 January 1851.

HARRINGTON, Harvey: Private, 27th U.S. Infantry Regiment, *Tigress*. Harrington was discharged at Detroit on 19 July 1815. He later applied for a pension on the basis that he failed to cover his ears during the battle, and because of this he was suffering pain and increasing deafness, with matter discharging from his ears; the pension request was denied. Harrington died in Licking County, Ohio in February of 1853 at age 57.

HARRISON, William Henry: Major General, U.S. Army. Harrison was born at Berkeley, Charles City County, Virginia on 9 February 1773. In April of 1791, at age 18, he was appointed an ensign in the U.S. Army, and he fought with General Anthony Wayne at Fallen Timbers on 20 August 1794. Harrison was elected a delegate to the U.S. Congress from the Northwest Territory in 1799, and the following year he was appointed governor of the new territory of Indiana; he was also made commander-in-chief of the territorial militia. Over the next 11 years he managed to negotiate 13 treaties with the Indians. Harrison was the victor at the Battle of the Tippecanoe River on 7 November 1811, often called the first battle of the War of 1812. Following his success at the Thames River he resigned his commission with the army. One year after the war ended, Harrison was elected to the U.S. House of Representatives from Ohio, and in 1824 he was elected to the U.S. Senate. In 1828 he was appointed Minister to the Republic of Columbia. Harrison was elected the ninth President of the United States in 1840, but he fell ill shortly after his 4 March 1841 inaugural speech. William Henry Harrison died on 4 April 1841.

HIGHT, William: Private, 147th Regiment of Pennsylvania Militia, *Scorpion*. After his discharge in November of 1813, Hight returned home to Juniata County, Pennsylvania. He married Jane Coder in Juniata County in July of 1820. In 1872, while a resident of Henderson Township, Huntingdon County, Pennsylvania, Hight applied for a pension on the basis of a wound received in his left calf during the battle. He was awarded an $8.00 per month pension commencing 14 April 1873.

The Battle of Lake Erie

HOLDUP (Stevens), Thomas: Lieutenant, U.S. Navy, *Trippe*. Holdup was born on 22 February 1795 in Charleston, South Carolina. He was living in a Charleston orphanage when General Daniel Stevens took an interest in his situation. In 1809 Stevens managed to obtain a midshipman's warrant for his protégé (in 1815 Holdup legally assumed the name of his benefactor, so during his early career he is listed as Holdup, while in later years he is found as Stevens). After serving on the *Hornet, President*, and *Constitution*, he was assigned to the *John Adams*, from which he was dispatched to the lakes in 1812. In December of 1812 he distinguished himself in an assault on a British battery opposite Black Rock; Holdup was wounded in the hand during this action. After his stint as commander of the *Trippe*, Holdup served as the *Niagara*'s first lieutenant during the campaign to recapture Fort Michilimackinac in the summer of 1814. He was promoted to lieutenant on 24 July 1813, to master commandant in 1825, and to captain in 1836. Stevens died on 21 January 1841 while in command of the Washington Navy Yard, leaving a wife and several children. U.S. Navy destroyers were named for Holdup Stevens in both World War I (DD-86) and World War II (DD-479).

INGLIS, George: Lieutenant, Royal Navy, *Detroit*. Born in 1787, Inglis was the son of Admiral John J. Inglis. He entered the Royal Navy as a second class volunteer on 27 August 1805. Over the next several years he served on blockade duty off the Netherlands port of Flushing and the French port of Brest. In 1812 Inglis was made a midshipman, and he was promoted to lieutenant while on board the *Royal George* on Lake Ontario on 25 March 1813. Inglis assumed command of the HMS *Detroit* after Barclay was wounded.

IRVINE, Robert: Lieutenant, Provincial Marine, *Queen Charlotte*. A Scot who was born in the Orkney Islands, Irvine's full name was Robert Irvine Crookshank; his reason for dropping his last name is unknown. Before the war Irvine worked for the Northwest Fur Company as master of the brig *Caledonia*, and he was still in command of the *Caledonia* when that vessel was captured off Fort Erie by Jesse Elliott on the night of 8/9 October 1812; during that engagement Irvine was wounded by a cutlass stroke. He was subsequently commissioned a second lieutenant in the Provincial Marine, and was later promoted to first lieutenant. At the River Raisin he was again wounded while in the process of capturing an American artillery piece. On Lake Erie he succeeded to command of the *Queen Charlotte* after Captain Finnis was killed and Lieutenant Stokoe was wounded. Irvine was an artist, and his watercolor of the larger combatant vessels at anchor in Put-in-Bay harbor after the battle is the only known contemporary rendering of any of the warships that fought in the engagement.

JOHNSON, James: Lieutenant Colonel, Kentucky Militia. Born in Orange County, Virginia on 1 January 1774, Johnson served in the Kentucky Senate from 1803 to 1811. He raised a company of Kentucky cavalry at the outset of the war, and later trained the regiment raised by his brother (see next) in the spring of 1813. Reportedly he was "a man of great dignity and suavity of manner." Johnson was a serving member of the U.S. House of Representatives when he died at Washington on 13 August 1826.

JOHNSON, Richard M.: Colonel, Kentucky Militia. Johnson was born at Floyd's Station in Jefferson County, Kentucky in 1780. He began practicing law at age 19, and he was elected to the Kentucky Legislature before his 21st birthday. After serving two terms he was elected as a republican to the U.S. Congress in 1806, eventually becoming a member of the

Roll of Honor

faction known as the war hawks. Johnson, retaining his seat in Congress, was appointed as an aide to General William Henry Harrison in the late summer of 1812, but he returned to Washington in November for the second session of Congress. Three months later he was authorized to raise a regiment of Kentucky mounted volunteers. In February of 1814, still unable to walk due to wounds suffered at the Battle of the Thames River, he set out for Washington to resume his seat in Congress. He voluntarily retired from the House of Representatives in 1819, but he was immediately elected to the U.S. Senate, where he remained until 1829. Following his tenure in the Senate, Johnson was once again elected to the U.S. House of Representatives and held the seat until 1836, when he became Vice President of the United States under Martin Van Buren. Returning to Kentucky in 1840, he was elected yet again to the U.S. House of Representatives. Johnson was still serving as a member of the House when he died at Frankfort, Kentucky on 19 November 1850.

JOHNSON, William: Boatswain's Mate, U.S. Navy, *Lawrence*. Discharged from the U.S. Navy on 24 March 1815, Johnson returned to his home in Philadelphia. On the date of his discharge he was awarded a disability pension of $6.00 per month. Still suffering from the effects of his wound in 1817, he was admitted to the Pennsylvania Hospital with "a pulmonary disease, occasioned by a wound, which he received in the naval action on Lake Erie." Johnson never recovered; he died in the hospital on 16 June 1818.

LANSFORD, James H.: Seaman, U.S. Navy, *Niagara*. Lansford was discharged at Erie on 23 May 1814. He traveled to Washington, where a surgeon advised him to have his unhealed wound attended to. Amazingly, Lansford refused and made his way to Baltimore, where he shipped on board the U.S. Frigate *Java*, commanded by Perry. However, his inflamed leg wound soon forced him to seek medical care. Lansford was placed on the pension rolls on 26 April 1816 and given a half-disability pension of $4.00 per month. He afterward resided in Portsmouth, Virginia.

LAUB, Henry: Midshipman, U.S. Navy, *Lawrence*. Killed in action on 10 September 1813, Laub was buried on South Bass Island. The destroyer USS *Laub* (DD 613) was named for him during World War II.

LUCAS, John: Private, 147th Regiment of Pennsylvania Militia, *Ariel*. Lucas was under a surgeon's care for six weeks after the battle. Following his release and discharge from the militia in November of 1813, Lucas was forced to limp home to Centre Country, Pennsylvania on his mangled foot. He later married Rachel Yarnell, with whom he fathered one son. John Lucas died on 27 September 1858 in Centre County.

MASON, Francis: Quartermaster's Mate, U.S. Navy, *Lawrence*. On 20 June 1814 a surgeon at the Washington Navy Yard avowed that Mason had "totally lost the use of his left arm, in consequence of a wound which he rec'd near the shoulder joint which is still open and the bone exfoliating, his case appears to rank among the highest grades of disability." Mason was subsequently issued a full disability pension.

MASON, Sanford A.: Sergeant, 28th U.S. Infantry Regiment, *Niagara*. Mason was discharged from the 28th U.S. Infantry on 23 April 1814, after which he applied for and was granted a full disability pension of $8.00 per month commencing 24 April 1814. Mason lived in Kentucky after the war.

The Battle of Lake Erie

MATTISON, Andrew: Seaman, U.S. Navy, *Lawrence*. On 16 June 1814 a surgeon at the Washington Navy Yard stipulated that Mattison's "leg was fractured during the action of the 10th of September 1813" and that because "his right leg is shorter than the other, he will remain lame for life." He was issued a $5.00 per month disability pension as of that date. Mattison returned to his home in Newport, Rhode Island, but in the early 1830's he moved to Gloucester, Massachusetts, where he still resided as late as December of 1838.

MAYS, Wilson: Carpenter's Mate, U.S. Navy, *Lawrence*. Killed in action on 10 September 1813, Mays was buried at sea near West Sister Island.

McMANOMY, George: Private, 28th U.S. Infantry Regiment, *Niagara*. Discharged from the army at Detroit on 30 June 1815, McManomy applied for and was awarded a three-quarters disability pension of $6.00 per month beginning 24 September 1823. A shoemaker born in Pennsylvania, McManomy lived in Fayette County, Kentucky after the war.

MILES, James: Seaman, U.S. Navy, *Lawrence*. From Portland, Maine (then Massachusetts), Miles enlisted in the U.S. Navy at New York on 27 May 1812 under the name of James Moses (he had been previously impressed into the Royal Navy but he deserted and enlisted in the U.S. Navy under a false name in the event of capture). Miles was sent to Lake Ontario in December of 1812. He fought at York on 27 April 1813 and Fort George on 27 May 1813; shortly thereafter he was sent to Lake Erie. On 11 September 1813, Surgeon's Mate Usher Parsons recorded in his diary:

> At 10 Oclock [sic] I amputated the arm of James Moses...This case was a compound fracture of the humerus within 2 inches of the head with a loss of some of the integuments. Was unable to apply the Tourniquette and used compression on the first rib. After dividing the bone, found the artery had retracted so much that it was 15 minutes before I could arrive to it and then only by dissection. Secured it and made a tolerable covering.

After his recovery Miles was promoted to Purser's Steward; he served on the Lake Erie Naval Station until his discharge on 23 April 1816. He immediately applied for and was granted a disability pension beginning 1 July 1816. Miles married Isabella Dougherty on 11 May 1820 at Millcreek, Erie County, Pennsylvania, where he resided until his death on 15 May 1853.

NEWEN, John: Quartermaster's Mate, U.S. Navy, *Lawrence*. On 12 September 1812, Surgeon's Mate Usher Parsons wrote in his diary that he "Trepanned [a trepan was a surgical tool used to cut and remove a small circular piece of bone from a patient's skull] John Newen, Q. Master, removed several pieces of bone from the cerebrum and a piece of leather hat. Found him sinking during the operation and dressed him immediately." John Newen died as a result of his wound on 17 September 1813.

PARSONS, Usher: Surgeon's Mate, U.S. Navy, *Lawrence*. Parsons was born at Alfred, Maine (then Massachusetts) on 18 August 1788. Having finished his medical studies by the time war was declared in 1812, he volunteered for the navy and was assigned to the *John Adams*. The entire crew of the *John Adams* was shipped to the Great Lakes, and Parsons was eventually ordered to Lake Erie. Parsons remained on the lakes until after the Mackinaw campaign in 1814, whereupon he rejoined Perry on board the U.S. Frigate *Java*. He later served on the U.S. Frigate *Guerriere* and also at the Charlestown Navy Yard before

Roll of Honor

resigning from the U.S. Navy. In 1822 Parsons married Mary J. Holmes, but she died three years later, leaving Parsons with a young son. Over succeeding years Parsons served as a professor at Brown University, as the president of the Rhode Island Medical Society, and he was the very first vice president of the National Medical Association. Parsons died on 19 December 1868, age 80, at Providence, Rhode Island.

PECKHAM, Isaac: Carpenter's Mate, U.S. Navy, *Caledonia*. Unable to work because of his leg injury, Peckham was issued a disability pension by the Navy Department. Despite his pension, Peckham, at age 81, was residing in a poor house in Middleton, Rhode Island in 1854.

PERRY, Oliver Hazard: Master Commandant, U.S. Navy, *Lawrence/Niagara*. Shortly after the Battle of the Thames, Perry transferred to the East Coast and resumed command of the gunboat flotilla at Newport. He had been promoted to captain as a result of the victory on Lake Erie, and in July of 1814 Perry was given command of the 44-gun frigate *Java*, then under construction at Baltimore. While engaged in fitting out the *Java*, Perry participated in the defense of both Washington and Baltimore during the late summer British invasion of the Chesapeake Bay region. The *Java* cruised the Mediterranean in 1815-1816, but upon the ship's return Perry became embroiled in controversy with the *Java*'s Marine officer, Captain John Heath, whom Perry had slapped during an unseemly incident. A duel was fought between Perry and Heath on 19 October 1817, but honor was satisfied without blood being shed. Strife continued to follow Perry's post-war career. An exchange of acrimonious letters induced Jesse Elliott to challenge Perry to a duel in 1818, but the victor of Lake Erie instead filed formal court-martial charges against his former subordinate. Not wishing to re-open old wounds, President James Monroe and Acting Secretary of the Navy Benjamin Homans quietly quashed the matter. To mollify and distract his contentious naval hero, Monroe selected Perry to oversee an important diplomatic mission to Venezuela and Argentina. Having completed the first stage of his assignment at Angostura, Venezuela, Perry has just re-boarded the USS *Nonsuch* to sail down the Orinoco River when he was felled by yellow fever. Perry died on board the *Nonsuch* on 23 August 1819, his 34th birthday. Buried at Port of Spain on the Island of Trinidad immediately after his death, Perry's body was exhumed in the autumn of 1826 and returned to the United States. The body was reinterred with a formal military burial at Newport, Rhode Island on 4 December 1826. Several U.S. Navy ships have been named for Perry over the years. The latest, a guided missile frigate (FFG-7), was decommissioned in 1997. *The Oliver Hazard Perry* was the prototype in a line of more than 50 "Perry" class frigates built by the navy.

POHIG, Charles: Seaman, U.S. Navy, *Lawrence*. Killed in action on 10 September 1813, he was buried at sea near West Sister Island.

PROCTER, Henry: Major General, British Army. The son of a British Army surgeon, Procter was born in Ireland in 1763. On 5 April 1781 he joined the 43rd Regiment of Foot as an ensign, but he rose quickly through the ranks via the purchase system, whereby junior officers were permitted to buy their way to a higher rank. Procter procured the rank of lieutenant in December 1781, captain in November 1792, and major in 1795. He received a merit promotion to lieutenant colonel on 9 October 1800 and transferred to the 41st Foot. In 1802 he was sent to Canada, where he was elevated to the rank of colonel on 25 July 1810. An able administrator, Procter commanded Fort George at the beginning of the War of 1812. Shortly after hostilities commenced he was ordered by General Isaac Brock to

The Battle of Lake Erie

assume command of the Right Division in the Western District of Upper Canada at Amherstburg. On 4 June 1813 he was promoted to major general as a result of his victory at the River Raisin on 22 January of that year. Procter was censured for his conduct at the Thames River, and a court-martial board ruled that he was "deficient in energy and judgement." Sentenced to a suspension of rank and pay for six months, the verdict was reduced to a public reprimand by the Prince Regent. Even so, Procter's career was ruined, and 1816 no longer found his name on the Army List. Procter retired to Bath, England, where he died at the age of 59 on 31 October 1822.

REEMS, John: Private, 28th U.S. Infantry Regiment, *Niagara*. Despite his wounds, Reems re-enlisted on 3 May 1814 for the duration. He was discharged at Detroit on 30 June 1815, after which he returned to Fleming County, Kentucky. There he married Sally Swim on 10 September 1816. Four years later he applied for a pension on the grounds that his arm had atrophied, plus complications from his head wound had caused paralysis and impaired speech; he received a two-thirds disability pension of $5.33 per month beginning 19 September 1820. Reems moved about, living in several places in Kentucky before relocating to Missouri in 1843. In 1854, the 72-year-old Reems was living near Fort Scott, Kansas.

ROLLETTE, Frederick: Lieutenant, Provincial Marine, *Lady Prevost*. Rollette was born in Quebec in 1783. Before joining the Provincial Marine, he served seven years with the Royal Navy, having entered service at an early age. Rollette fought with Lord Horatio Nelson's squadrons at both the Nile, where he received multiple wounds, and at Trafalgar. He was commissioned a second lieutenant in the Provincial Marine on 4 October 1807, and was promoted to first lieutenant and command of the brig *General Hunter* on 25 April 1812. Rollette was the officer who captured the packet *Cuyahoga* (General William Hull's supply vessel) on 3 July 1812, and he acted as an artillery officer at the River Raisin, where he was wounded in the head by a musket ball. During the Battle of Lake Erie, when Lieutenant Buchan was wounded, Rollette assumed command of the *Lady Prevost* until he was himself severely wounded. Rollette never fully recovered from his injuries, and he died in Quebec on 17 March 1831 at age 48, leaving a wife and several children in destitute condition.

SILHAMMER, John: Private, 147th Regiment of Pennsylvania Militia, *Scorpion*. A saddler from Bellefonte, Pennsylvania, Silhammer was killed in action on 10 September 1813; he was buried at sea near West Sister Island.

SCHOFIELD, George: Private, 28th U.S. Infantry Regiment, *Niagara*. Schofield died on South Bass Island on 20 September 1813, most likely as a result of wounds suffered on 10 September 1813. Schofield may have been the individual that Parsons described in his surgical account of the battle. In that narrative Parsons wrote:

> ...a canister shot, twice the size of a musket ball, entered the eye, and on the fifth or sixth day, was detected at the inside of the angle of the lower jaw, and cut out. In its passage, it must have fractured the orbitar plate of the superior maxillary bone, the orbito-temporal process of the splenoid bone, and passing under the temporal arch, inside the coronal process of the lower jaw, must have done great injury to the temporal muscle and other soft parts lying in its way.

The surgeon's mate further related that the man in question was a Kentucky rifleman, and that he lost his right eye. Parsons might have been referring to Joshua Trapnell, but Trapnell had died by the time the casualty report was compiled. This could also have been John

Roll of Honor

Reems, but Reems made no mention about the loss of an eye in his pension request, and it is doubtful if Reems would have been allowed to re-enlist having lost an eye. Schofield died ten days after the battle, so the Kentuckian that Parsons described was probably Schofield.

SCHROUDER, John: Ordinary Seaman, U.S. Navy, *Lawrence*. The severity of his wound caused Schrouder's right arm to be amputated near the shoulder. On 31 May 1867, at age 82, Schrouder was living in Albany, New York and receiving a disability pension of $6.00 per month.

SERGEANT, Hosea: Private, 17th U.S. Infantry Regiment, *Lawrence*. From Wells, Maine (then Massachusetts), Sergeant was born on 10 January 1795. He went to sea in the merchant trade at age 15 and found himself in New Orleans when war was declared. On 18 March 1813, in the process of working his way home overland, Sergeant enlisted in the 17th U.S. Infantry at Paris, Kentucky. He was at Fort Stephenson when the call came for volunteers for the Lake Erie squadron, and he rejoined his regiment nine days after the battle. He was later promoted, becoming Sergeant Sergeant, before being discharged at Fort Erie on 30 November 1814. After returning to his home in Maine he married and raised a family. The Sergeants eventually moved to the Boston area, possibly to Cambridge, where Hosea died in 1868.

SLOSS, William: Landsman, U.S. Navy, *Ariel*. When Sloss applied for a pension in 1826, a surgeon asserted that the original splinter wound to his breast was slight and that Sloss's current health problems were not attributable to his wound. Sloss apparently lived in Erie, Pennsylvania after the war.

SMITH, William: Private, 26th U.S. Infantry Regiment, *Ariel*. Despite his injuries, Smith remained with the 26th U.S. after the engagement. He was promoted to sergeant on 11 November 1813, but he deserted while at Geneva, New York on 23 March 1814 (apparently there were no repercussions because of his desertion). In 1824 Smith applied for a pension. After an examination, two surgeons certified that he was "crippled in both his hands by an injury which the tendons of the fingers have received whereby they are (especially the tendons of the two smaller fingers of both hands) permanently contracted so as to render him incapable of opening either hand..." A pension of $8.00 per month was awarded on 9 May 1825. Smith lived with his wife, six sons, and three daughters in Hamilton, Ohio.

STOKOE, Thomas: Lieutenant, Royal Navy, *Queen Charlotte*. Stokoe assumed command of the *Queen Charlotte* after Commander Finnis was killed, but he was shortly thereafter wounded by a wood splinter and forced to relinquish command.

TAYLOR, William Vigneron: Sailing Master, U.S. Navy, *Lawrence*. Of French descent, Taylor was born at Newport, Rhode Island on 11 April 1780. Prior to the war he was a master in the merchant service, but Taylor joined the U.S. Navy in 1813 at the behest of Perry. He was commissioned a lieutenant in 1814, promoted to commander in 1831, and to captain in 1841. Among his numerous postings during a long career was that of captain of the USS *Ohio*, a 74-gun line-of-battle ship that he sailed around Cape Horn in his 68th year. Taylor returned to Newport after he retired, where on 9 February 1858 he was felled by a stroke; he died two days later. Taylor was survived by his wife and four children. U.S. Navy destroyers were named for Taylor in both World War I (DD 94) and World War II (DD 468).

The Battle of Lake Erie

THOMPSON, William: Seaman, U.S. Navy, *Lawrence*. Surgeon's Mate Usher Parsons amputated Thompson's left leg on 10 September 1813. After recovering from his wound he returned to New York, where on 23 May 1814 Thompson was awarded a $6.00 per month Navy pension.

TRAPNELL, Joshua: Private, 17th U.S. Infantry Regiment, *Niagara*. From Baltimore, Maryland, Trapnell died as a result of wounds suffered in battle on 10 September 1813. His wife, Elizabeth, was subsequently awarded a $3.50 per month widow's pension.

TURNER, Daniel: Lieutenant, U.S. Navy, *Caledonia*. A native of New York, Turner was warranted a midshipman on 1 January 1808, and elevated to lieutenant on 12 March 1813. When assigned to Lake Erie he commanded the *Niagara* for a brief period before being superceded by Jesse Elliott and transferred to the *Caledonia*. Turner was in command of the *Scorpion* when the British captured the little schooner on Lake Huron on the night of 5 September 1814. After the war Turner rejoined Perry on board the newly built U.S. Frigate *Java* for a cruise to the Mediterranean, after which he fought pirates in the West Indies. He was promoted to master commandant in March of 1825, and to captain in March of 1835. Known as a strict disciplinarian, Turner's distinguished career included a stint as captain of the U.S. Frigate *Constitution*, commodore of the Pacific squadron, and command of the Portsmouth, New Hampshire Navy Yard. On 23 May 1837 Turner married Catherine Bryan in Philadelphia, a union that produced one daughter, Leota Kate. Turner died in Philadelphia from heart disease on 4 February 1850. The U.S. Navy named three destroyers (DD 249, DD 648 and DD 834) to commemorate Daniel Turner's service.

VAN DYKE, Charles: Ordinary Seaman, U.S. Navy, *Lawrence*. A few months after the engagement, Surgeon's Mate Usher Parsons reported that Van Dyke had "received a splinter wound in the leg, of which he was nearly cured by the first of October..." Even so, Van Dyke applied for and was awarded a $5.00 per month pension commencing 27 May 1814. In 1822, while living in New York City, Van Dyke appeared before a group of physicians. The doctors attested to the fact that Van Dyke had "been wounded severely in the right leg, by musket balls and cannister [sic] shot," and that he was still entitled to his pension. Van Dyke died sometime in 1824, probably in March, leaving his wife and two children destitute.

VARNUM, George: Seaman, U.S. Navy, *Lawrence*. On 11 September 1813, Surgeon's Mate Usher Parsons wrote in his diary, "After breakfast I amputated the leg of George Varnum of Wiscasset [Maine, then Massachusetts]." As a result of his disability, Varnum was awarded a $6.00 per month navy pension commencing on 23 May 1814. Varnum's pension file contains an appeal to the Secretary of the Navy, dated 1 August 1822 from New York City. The letter stipulates that, " I have a wife and five children who are suffering on acct. of my misfortune, my wife has lost her health...the Navy Department ought to consider my case...and thereby prevent me and my family from becoming paupers." It is uncertain whether or not the navy acted on Varnum's request.

WILKINSON, Asel: Pilot, U.S. Navy, *Ariel*. After the war Wilkinson lived in the Buffalo, New York area before moving to Colden, Erie County, New York. He married Alvina McKay on 25 May 1851, apparently his second marriage. On 4 July 1861 Wilkinson was attending holiday festivities in Buffalo when he collapsed and died.

Roll of Honor

WOOD, Eleazor: Major, U.S. Army. In 1806, Wood was 17th in his graduating class at the newly established U.S. Military Academy at West Point. During the first year of the war, as an engineer on the staff of General William Henry Harrison, he supervised construction of Fort Meigs and Fort Stephenson. Wood received a brevet promotion to major as a result of his engineering skills and for conspicuous service while commanding an artillery battery during the first siege of Fort Meigs. After the Battle of the Thames River, Wood was transferred to the staff of General Jacob Brown, where he fought as an engineer and artillery officer during the 1814 Niagara campaign. On 17 September 1814, Wood led an assault column against the besieging British forces at Fort Erie, but he was mortally wounded during the British counterattack. Brown was so impressed with Wood's abilities that he personally paid for a monument to be erected at West Point to honor the fallen engineer. A coastal defense fort constructed in New York harbor was later named for Eleazor Wood. Situated on Bedloe's Island, the brick fortification now serves as the base for the Statue of Liberty.

YARNALL, John Joliffe: Lieutenant, U.S. Navy, *Lawrence*. A Pennsylvania native, Yarnall was living in Wheeling, West Virginia (then Virginia) when he was warranted a midshipman in the U.S. Navy in 1809. Upon joining the U.S. Brig *Enterprise*, Yarnall embarked upon a 26-month cruise that circumnavigated the globe. He was commissioned a lieutenant in July of 1813. Following the battle, Yarnall was placed in command of the *Lawrence*, which returned to Erie in the capacity of a hospital ship; shortly thereafter he received orders to report to the 28-gun corvette *John Adams*. Yarnall was later posted to the U.S. Brig *Epervier*, which was lost at sea with all hands during the late summer of 1815. During World War II a U.S. Navy destroyer (DD 541) was named in honor of Yarnall.

ENDNOTES

[1] John Armstrong to William Henry Harrison, 4 March 1813, in Richard C. Knopf (ed.), *Document Transcriptions of the War of 1812 in the Northwest* (Columbus: Ohio Historical Society, 1957), 10 volumes, Volume 8, 138. The correct name for the fort at Amherstburg during the War of 1812 was Fort Amherstburg. The second fort, built following the war, was dubbed Fort Malden. Still, throughout the course of the war Americans commonly referred to the picketed earthwork as Malden, and even the occasional Canadian called it Fort Malden, so at the time of the War of 1812 the designations were inter-changeable. Since references to the town of Amherstburg, the Amherstburg Navy Yard, and Fort Amherstburg can become very confusing, the fortification will herein be referred to as Fort Malden.

[2] Frank H. Severance, "Career Of Daniel Dobbins," in *Publications of the Buffalo Historical Society, Volume VIII* (Buffalo: Buffalo Historical Society, 1905), 260-262.

[3] Robert D. Ilisevich, *Daniel Dobbins, Frontier Mariner* (Erie: Erie County Historical Society, 1993), 17-20.

[4] Severance, "Career Of Daniel Dobbins," 261-262; Secretary of the Navy Paul Hamilton to Commodore Thomas Tingey, 15 September 1812, in William S. Dudley (ed.), *The Naval War of 1812, A Documentary History*, (Washington, D.C., 1985), Volume I, 309; Hamilton to Dobbins, 15 September 1812, in op. cit., 310.

[5] Hamilton to Dobbins, 15 September 1812, in op. cit., 310; Jesse D. Elliott to Dobbins, 2 October 1812, in op. cit., 321; Elliott to Isaac Chauncey, 14 September 1812, in op. cit., 312-314; Chauncey to New York Governor Daniel Tomkins, 24 September 1812, in Letterbooks of Isaac Chauncey, William L. Clements Library, University of Michigan, Ann Arbor (hereafter WLCL).

[6] Chauncey to Hamilton, 8 October 1812, 27 October 1813, Chauncey Letterbooks, WLCL.

[7] Hamilton to Dobbins, 15 September 1812, in Dudley (ed.), *The Naval War of 1812*, Volume I, 310; Dobbins to Hamilton, 12 December 1813, in Severance, "Career Of Daniel Dobbins," 266-267.

[8] Chauncey to Hamilton, 1 January 1813, to Dobbins, 9 January 1813, Chauncey Letterbooks, WLCL.

[9] Chauncey to Noah Brown, 18 February 1813, Chauncey Letterbooks, WLCL.

[10] Chauncey to James Sackett, 24 February 1813, Chauncey Letterbooks, WLCL.

[11] Chauncey to Augustus Porter, 22 April 1813, Chauncey Letterbooks, WLCL. Porter was the Navy Agent at Buffalo. Chauncey wrote to Porter informing him that the riggers were on their way from Sackets Harbor to Erie and directing him to facilitate the riggers' passage in whatever way possible.

[12] Perry to Hamilton, 6 June 1812, Records of the Department of the Navy (RG45), Masters Commandant Letters, U.S. National Archives and Records

Notes

Administration (hereafter NARA).

[13] Hamilton to Perry, 6 October 1812, Records of the Department of the Navy, Letters to Officers, Ships of War, NARA.

[14] Perry to Hamilton, 28 November 1812, Masters Commandant Letters, NARA; Chauncey to Perry, 20 January 1813, Chauncey Letterbooks, WLCL. Perry's letter to Chauncey was not found, but Chauncey's 20 January missive states that the commodore "...arrived [at Sackets Harbor] yesterday from Buffaloe [sic] and found [Perry's] favor of the 1st inst...."

[15] Chauncey to Perry, 20 January 1813, Chauncey Letterbooks, WLCL.

[16] Chauncey to Secretary of the Navy William Jones, 21 January 1813, Chauncey Letterbooks, WLCL; Perry to Jones, 17 February 1813, Masters Commandant Letters, NARA; "List of Officers & Men from Newport, R.I. under command of Captain O.H. Perry," Oliver Hazard Perry Papers, WLCL.

[17] Chauncey to Jones, 16 March 1813, Chauncey Letterbooks, WLCL.

[18] Max Rosenberg, *The Building of Perry's Fleet on Lake Erie, 1812-1813* (Harrisburg: Pennsylvania Historical and Museum Commission, 1968), 12. Spencer Tucker, *Arming The Fleet, U.S. Navy Ordnance in the Muzzle Loading Era* (Annapolis: Naval Institute Press, 1989), 63-64. The carronades for the Lake Erie squadron were cast by Henry Foxall at the Columbia Foundry in Georgetown, D.C.

[19] Perry to Brigadier General William H. Winder, 18 April 1813, Perry Papers, WLCL.

[20] Chauncey to Jones, 24 February 1813, Chauncey Letterbooks, WLCL; General Order, 31 March 1813, in "Executive Minutes of Governor Simon Snyder," in Gertrude MacKinney (ed.), *Pennsylvania Archives, Ninth Series*, Volume V, 1812-1814 (Harrisburg: John R. Hood, Director, Bureau of Publications, 1931), 3344-3345.

[21] Perry to Chauncey, 7 May 1813, Perry Papers, WLCL; Simon Snyder to John Armstrong, 1 April 1813, in John B. Linn & Wm. H. Egle, (ed.), *Pennsylvania Archives, Second Series*, Volume XII, (Harrisburg, Clarence M. Busch, State Printer of Pennsylvania, 1896), 649.

[22] Chauncey to Jones, 5 March 1813, Chauncey Letterbooks, WLCL.

[23] Muster Rolls of Lieutenant John Brooks' detachment of U.S. Marines, Records of the U.S. Marine Corps (RG127), NARA; U.S. Marine Corps Size Rolls, Op.Cit.

[24] Gerard T. Altoff, "Leathernecks On Lake Erie," in *Leatherneck*, Volume LXXI, Number 11, November 1988, 36-43.

[25] Muster rolls of Lieutenant John Brooks' detachment of U.S. Marines, U.S. Marine Corps Size Rolls; NARA; muster rolls of Colonel Rees Hill's 147th Regiment of Pennsylvania Militia, Muster Rolls of Volunteer Organizations, War of 1812, Records of the Adjutant General's Office (RG94), NARA; Compiled Service Records of Volunteer Soldiers Who Served during the War of 1812, op. cit.; War of 1812 Pension Application Files, Records of the Pension Office (RG15),

NARA; muster rolls of Pennsylvania units that served at Erie in 1813, in Thomas L. Montgomery (ed.), *Pennsylvania Archives, Series Six*, (Harrisburg, Harrisburg Publishing Co., State Printer, 1907), Vols. VII, IX, and X.

[26] Chauncey to Jones, 29 May 1813, Chauncey Letterbooks, WLCL.

[27] Perry to Jones, 19 June 1813, 24 June 1813, Masters Commandant Letters, NARA.

[28] Frank H. Severance (ed.), "The Dobbins Papers," in *Publications of the Buffalo Historical Society, Volume VIII* (Buffalo: Buffalo Historical Society, 1905), 320-321; Alexander S. Mackenzie, *Commodore Perry, His Life & Achievements* (Akron, Ohio: J.K. Richardson & Sons, 1910), 112; Richard Dillon, *We Have Met The Enemy* (New York: McGraw-Hill, 1978), 94.

[29] Levi Hukill to Perry, 23 June 1813, Harrison to Perry, 5 July 1813, A. H. Holmes to Perry, 23 July 1813, Perry Papers, WLCL; Perry to Jones 15 July 1813, 19 July 1813, Masters Commandant Letters, NARA. Hukill was Harrison's Assistant Inspector General, while Holmes was the Assistant Adjutant General.

[30] Chauncey to Perry, 15 March 1813, to Jones, 16 March 1813, Chauncey Letterbooks, WLCL.

[31] Perry to Chauncey, 9 May 1813, 22 May 1813, Perry Papers, WLCL.

[32] Chauncey to Jones, 17 July 1813, Chauncey Letterbooks, WLCL; Perry to Chauncey, 27 June 1813, Perry Letterbook, op. cit.

[33] Chauncey to Jones, 4 June 1813, Chauncey Letterbooks, WLCL.

[34] Chauncey to Jones, 16 May 1813, 29 May 1813, 4 June 1813, 17 June 1813, 1 July 1813, 10 July 1813, and 17 July 1813, Chauncey Letterbooks, WLCL.

[35] Chauncey to Jones, 29 May 1813, 4 June 1813, Chauncey Letterbooks, WLCL; Jones to Chauncey, 9 July 1813, Records of the Department of the Navy, Private Letters, NARA.

[36] Jones to Perry, 25 May 1813, Letters to Officers, Ships of War, NARA; Perry to Jones, 24 June 1813, Masters Commandant Letters, NARA; Jones to Chauncey, 3 July 1813, in William S. Dudley (ed.), *The Naval War of 1812, A Documentary History*, (Washington, D.C., Naval Historical Center, 1992), Volume II, 509-512.

[37] Perry to Jones, 24 June 1813, Masters Commandant Letters, NARA.

[38] Jones to Chauncey, 3 July 1813, in Dudley (ed.), *The Naval War of 1812, Volume II*, 509-512; Chauncey to Perry, 30 July 1813, Chauncey Letterbooks, WLCL.

[39] Perry to Jones, 27 July 1813, 30 July 1813, Masters Commandant Letters, NARA; Perry to Chauncey, 27 July 1813, Perry Papers, WLCL.

[40] Christopher McKee, *A Gentlemanly and Honorable Profession, The Creation of the U.S. Naval Officer Corps, 1794-1815* (Annapolis: Naval Institute Press, 1991), 233; "List of Officers and Men from Newport, R.I. under command of O.H. Perry," Perry Papers, WLCL; Gerard T. Altoff, *Amongst My Best Men: African Americans and the War of 1812* (Put-in-Bay, Ohio: The Perry Group, 1996), 20-21, 35-43; Altoff, *Deep Water Sailors–Shallow Water Soldiers: Manning the United*

Notes

States Fleet on Lake Erie, 1813 (Put-in-Bay, Ohio: The Perry Group, 1993), 13-14. The latter work was originally published in serialized form in *Inland Seas*, the journal of The Great Lakes Historical Society, from Spring 1990 through Fall 1991.

[41] "Account of the Battle of Lake Erie," affidavit by William V. Taylor, 23 June 1818, Perry Papers, WLCL; Samuel Hambleton diaries, entry of 12 October 1812, Maryland Historical Society; anonymous letter, dateline "Meadville (Pa.), 6 April 1846," in Maria Campbell and James Freeman Clark, *Revolutionary Services and Civil Life of General William Hull* (New York: D. Appleton & Co., 1848), 470. Taylor reported that many of the reinforcements sent from Lake Ontario "were barely able to assist themselves," while Hambleton wrote that the "force consisted principally of the refuse of Commodore Chauncey's fleet." Elliott purportedly related at a later date that he was the officer who had the responsibility for selecting the men for Lake Erie, and that none but the worst were sent. See Altoff, *Deep Water Sailors–Shallow Water Soldiers*, 14-24.

[42] Muster rolls of Colonel Rees Hill's 147th Regiment of Pennsylvania Militia, Muster Rolls of Volunteer Organizations, War of 1812, NARA; muster rolls of the 17th, 132nd, 133rd, 134th, 135th, 136th, 137th, and 147th Pennsylvania Militia Regiments, in *Pennsylvania Archives, Series Six*, Volumes VII, IX, and X; muster rolls of Lieutenant John Brooks' detachment of U.S. Marines, U.S. Marine Corps Muster Rolls, NARA; U.S. Marine Corps Size Rolls, op. cit.

[43] Perry to Jones, 22 July 1813, 30 July 1813, Masters Commandant Letters, NARA; Rosenberg, *Building of Perry's Fleet*, 50.

[44] Dillon, *We Have Met The Enemy*, 109; Rosenberg, *Building of Perry's Fleet*, 50-51.

[45] Severance (ed.), "The Dobbins Papers," 333.

[46] Oscar Jewell Harvey and Ernest Gray Smith, *A History Of Wilkes-Barre, Luzerne County, Pennsylvania* (Wilkes-Barre, 1927), 4 Volumes, Volume III, 1787.

[47] "Extracts taken from the court-martial proceedings of Robert Heriot Barclay," in Knopf (ed.), *Document Transcriptions of the War of 1812*, Volume IV, "Anecdotes of the Lake Erie Area, War of 1812," 1-14. Barclay's court-martial was conducted on board HMS *Gladiator* at the Portsmouth Navy Yard in England on 9 September 1814. A transcription of the entire court-martial can be found in the Canadian Public Archives in Ottawa, Canada.

[48] Ibid.; Rosenberg, *Building of Perry's Fleet*, 50-52.

[49] Perry to Jones, 4 August 1813, Masters Commandant Letters, NARA; pay and muster rolls for regiments of the 1st Brigade, 16th Division of Pennsylvania Militia called up for two weeks during late July and early August 1813, in *Pennsylvania Archives, Series 6*, Volume 10, 141-243; "List of known Pennsylvania Militiamen who volunteered to serve on board the U.S. Fleet for a forty-eight hour cruise during early August, 1813," in Altoff, *Deep Water Sailors – Shallow Water Soldiers*, 111-114.

---

[50] Perry to Jones, 4 August 1813, 11 August 1813, Masters Commandant Letters, NARA; Chauncey to Elliott, 3 August 1813, Chauncey Letterbooks, WLCL; Severance (ed.), "The Dobbins Papers," 334-335.

[51] Chauncey to Elliott, 7 September 1812, in Russell Jarvis, *A Biographical Notice of Com. Jesse D. Elliott; Containing A Review Of The Controversy Between Him And The Late Commodore Perry And A History Of The Figure-Head Of The U.S. Frigate Constitution* (Philadelphia: Printed For The Author, 1835), 16-17.

[52] Jarvis, *A Biographical Notice of Com. Jesse D. Elliott*, 26.

[53] Perry to Jones, 10 August 1813, Masters Commandant Letters, NARA.

[54] Perry to Jones, 21 August 1813, 2 September 1813, Masters Commandant Letters, NARA.

[55] Harrison to Armstrong, 15 September 1813, in *Document Transcriptions of the War of 1812*, Volume VII, Part 3, 78.

[56] "Prologue to Victory, General Orders, Fort Meigs to Put-in-Bay, April-September, 1813," in Kentucky Historical Society Register, Volume 60, 30.

[57] Muster Rolls of Regular Army Organizations—War of 1812, Register of Enlistments in the United States Army—War of 1812, Returns From United States Military Posts, Compiled Service Records of Volunteer Soldiers Who Served During the War of 1812, NARA; War of 1812 Pension Application Files, NARA; Lee A. Wallace Jr., "The Petersburg Volunteers," in Virginia Magazine of History, Number 82 (October 1974), 480.

[58] Ibid.

[59] Ibid.; "Samuel Hambleton's account of the Distribution of prize money on Lake Erie," in "Documents, Legislative and Executive, of the Congress of the United States," in *American State Papers, Naval Affairs*, Series IV, Volume 1, Washington: Gales and Seaton, 1834), 566-572; Altoff, *Deep Water Sailors—Shallow Water Soldiers*, 37-40.

[60] Barclay court-martial proceedings, in *Document Transcriptions of The War of 1812*, Volume IV, 9; Barclay to Sir James Lucas Yeo, 12 October 1813, in op. cit., 41.

[61] Op. cit., 1-14.

[62] Dulaney Forrest's account of the Battle of Lake Erie, written at Washington, D.C., 29 January 1821, in Perry Papers, WLCL; Charles J. Dutton, *Oliver Hazard Perry* (New York: Longmans, Green and Co., 1935), 144.

[63] "List of Killed and Wounded on board of the United States' squadron, under Command of O.H. Perry, Esq. in the Battle of 10th September 1813," in *American State Papers,* Part 1, Volume XIV, 295-296.

[64] "'Sloop of War *Lawrence* Journal,' 31 July 1813 - 28 September 1813," entry of 10 September 1813, in William V. Taylor Papers, Newport Historical Society. It was not unusual for both the captain and the ship's sailing master to keep a log, and Taylor apparently maintained a duplicate or possibly even the original of the *Lawrence*'s log.

Notes

---

[65] "General Order, U.S.S. *Lawrence*, off Sandusky, 21 August 1813," Order Book of Oliver Hazard Perry, Perry Papers, WLCL.

[66] See Gerard T. Altoff, "A Bulldog of a Naval Gun, The Carronade and its Impact on Lake Erie," in *The Journal of Erie Studies*, Spring 1998.

[67] Dutton, *Oliver Hazard Perry*, 145; Mackenzie, *Commodore Perry*, 171-172.

[68] Severance (ed.), "The Dobbins Papers," 343-344.

[69] O. H. Perry to Christopher Perry, 9 August 1813, Perry Papers, WLCL; Chauncey to Jones, 10 June 1813, Chauncey Letterbooks, WLCL; Barclay to Procter, 29 June 1813, in Dudley (ed.), *The Naval War of 1812,* Volume II, 483-485; Chauncey to Jones, 3 July 1813, in op. cit., 509-512; William V. Taylor to Abby Taylor; 15 September 1813, William V. Taylor Papers, NHS; Frederick C. Drake, "Artillery and Its Influence on Naval Tactics: Reflections on the Battle of Lake Erie," in William Jeffrey Welsh and David Curtis Skaggs (eds.), *War On The Great Lakes: Essays Commemorating the 175th Anniversary of the Battle of Lake Erie* (Kent, Ohio: The Kent State University Press, 1991) 17-29; Robert J. Dodge, *Battle of Lake Erie* (Fostoria, Ohio: Gray Printing Company, 1967), 15-17; Theodore Roosevelt, *Naval War of 1812* (New York: G.P. Putnam's Sons, 1882), 260-261. No two works, including contemporary writings, which compile the British and American armament agree. Prior to the battle, guns were constantly being transferred to and from the various vessels of both squadrons, and different sources offer inconsistent numbers, so the statistics used herein are an extrapolation. Although a number of sources were consulted, Dodge and Roosevelt were primarily used to extract the American numbers, while Drake's figures were the principal source for the British. The statistics Drake developed for the American squadron are inaccurate in relation to the sloop *Trippe*. Drake assigns the small sloop a 32-pounder long gun, but documentation in Oliver Hazard Perry's Order Book, found in the William L. Clements library, clearly specify that 24-pounder cannonballs were transferred to the *Trippe*, while other primary and secondary sources also show the *Trippe* mounting a 24-pounder. Broadside weight is another area of controversy concerning the two squadrons. Both flotillas mounted a number of guns on pivot mounts, which could fire from either larboard or starboard broadside. However, sources disagree on the number of pivot mounts for both squadrons. Also, sources vary as to the carronade mounted on the *Scorpion*; some state it was a 32-pounder while others stipulate a 24-pounder. It does appear odd, though not unreasonable, that only one 24-pounder carronade would appear on the U.S. squadron armament list. On 10 June 1813 Chauncey sent Secretary Jones a return of the armament on board the Lake Erie flotilla and no 24-pounder carronades were listed. If the flotilla did have a 24-pounder carronade, it would have made more sense to mount it on board the *Caledonia*, which already carried two long 24-pounders; the *Caledonia* mounted a 32-pounder carronade.

[70] Ibid.

[71] Kenneth Poolman, *Guns Off Cape Ann* (London: Rand, McNally & Co., 1961), 120.

The Battle of Lake Erie

[72] David C. Bunnell, *Travels and Adventures of David C. Bunnell During Twenty-Three Years of a Seafaring Life* (Palmyra, NY: J.H. Bortles Printer, 1831), 113.

[73] A number of primary and secondary sources were utilized to extrapolate the account of the battle, and the principal references will be listed here on a one-time basis. Among the primary sources referenced were: Samuel Hambleton diaries, Maryland Historical Society; Usher Parsons, "A Diary Kept During The Expedition To Lake Erie, Under Captain O.H. Perry, 1812-1814," Rhode Island Historical Society; Parsons, "Surgical Account of the Naval engagement on Lake Erie on the 10th September 1813,: in New England Journal of Medicine and Surgery, Volume 7, # 4, October 1818, 313-316; Parsons, *Battle of Lake Erie, A Discourse Delivered Before the Rhode Island Historical Society* on February 16, 1853 (Palmyra, NY: Benjamin T. Albro, Printer, 1854); William V. Taylor Papers, Newport Historical Society; accounts of the Battle of Lake Erie by Thomas Breese, Thomas Brownell, Stephen Champlin, Dulaney Forrest, Usher Parsons, Thomas Holdup Stevens, and Daniel Turner, in the Oliver Hazard Perry Papers, WLCL; *Document Transcriptions of the War of 1812 in the Northwest* (Columbus: Ohio Historical Society, 1957), 10 volumes, Volume IV; David C. Bunnell, *Travels and Adventures of David C. Bunnell During Twenty-Three Years of a Seafaring Life* (Palmyra, NY: J.H. Bortles Printer, 1831); William S. Dudley (ed.), *The Naval War of 1812, A Documentary History*, (Washington, D.C., 1992), 2 volumes; Jesse D. Elliott, *Speech of Com. Jesse Duncan Elliott, U.S.N. Delivered in Hagerstown, MD, on November 14, 1843* (Philadelphia: G.B. Zieber & Company, 1844); Frank H. Severance (ed.), "The Dobbins Papers," in *Publications of the Buffalo Historical Society*, Volume VIII (Buffalo: Buffalo Historical Society, 1905). Secondary sources include Gerard T. Altoff, *Deep Water Sailors, Shallow Water Soldiers: Manning the United States Fleet On Lake Erie - 1813* (Put-in-Bay, Ohio: The Perry Group, 1993); Altoff, *Amongst My Best Men, African-Americans and the War of 1812*, (Put-in-Bay, Ohio: The Perry Group, 1996); Tristam Burges, *Battle of Lake Erie With Notices of Commodore Elliot's [sic] Conduct In That Engagement* (Providence: Brown & Cady, 1839); James Fenimore Cooper, *History of the Navy of the United States of America* (Philadelphia: Lea and Blanchard, 1840), 2 volumes; Richard Dillon, *We Have Met The Enemy* (New York: McGraw-Hill, 1978); Captain W.W. Dobbins, *History of the Battle of Lake Erie and Reminiscences of the Flagships "Lawrence" and "Niagara"* (Erie: Ashby Printing Co., 1913); Robert J. Dodge, *Battle of Lake Erie* (Fostoria, Ohio: Gray Printing Company, 1967); Charles J. Dutton, *Oliver Hazard Perry* (New York: Longmans, Green and Co., 1935); Russell Jarvis, *A Biographical Notice of Com. Jesse D. Elliott; Containing A Review Of The Controversy Between Him And The Late Commodore Perry And A History Of The Figure-Head Of The U.S. Frigate Constitution* (Philadelphia: Printed For The Author, 1835); Benson J. Lossing, *The Pictorial Field-Book of the War of 1812* (New York: Harper & Brothers, Publishers, 1868); Olin L. Lyman, *Commodore Oliver Hazard Perry and the War*

Notes

on the Lakes (New York: New Amsterdam Book Co., 1905); Alexander Slidell Mackenzie, *Commodore Perry, His Life & Achievements* (Akron, Ohio: J.K. Richardson & Sons, 1910) centennial edition; Alfred Thayer Mahan, *Sea Power In Its Relations To The War of 1812* (New York: Greenwood Press, Publishers 1968), 2 volumes; James Cooke Mills, *Oliver Hazard Perry and the Battle of Lake Erie* (Detroit: John Philps, 1913); John N. Niles, *The Life of Oliver Hazard Perry* (Hartford: William S. Marsh, 1820); Theodore Roosevelt, *Naval War of 1812* (New York: G.P. Putnam's Sons, 1882); Frank H. Severance (ed.), "Career Of Daniel Dobbins," in *Publications of the Buffalo Historical Society, Volume VIII* (Buffalo: Buffalo Historical Society, 1905); David Curtis Skaggs and Gerard T. Altoff, *A Signal Victory, The Lake Erie Campaign, 1812-1813* (Annapolis: Naval Institute Press, 1997); William Jeffrey Welsh and David Curtis Skaggs (eds.), *War On The Great Lakes: Essays Commemorating the 175th Anniversary of the Battle of Lake Erie* (Kent, Ohio: The Kent State University Press, 1991).

[74] Accounts of the Battle of Lake Erie by Thomas Breese, Thomas Brownell, Stephen Champlin, Thomas Holdup Stevens, William V. Taylor, and Daniel Turner, Perry Papers, WLCL.

[75] Testimony of Lieutenant John J. Yarnall at the Court of Inquiry held in New York on 24 April 1815 to investigate the actions of Jesse D. Elliott on 10 September 1813, in Jarvis, *A Biographical Notice Of Com. Jesse D. Elliott*, 435-437.

[76] Accounts of the Battle of Lake Erie by Breese, Brownell, Champlin, Holdup Stevens, Taylor, and Turner, Perry Papers, WLCL; Jarvis, *A Biographical Notice Of Com. Jesse D. Elliott*, 33. Both the *Lawrence* and *Niagara* were pierced with 11 gun ports per side, but the forward port was normally kept open.

[77] "General Order, U.S.S. *Lawrence*," (no date, but recorded chronologically between 4 September and 9 September 1813), Perry Order Book, Perry Papers, WLCL.

[78] Account of the Battle of Lake Erie by William V. Taylor, Taylor Papers, NHS; Burges, *Battle of Lake Erie*, 28.

[79] Sworn testimony of Midshipman Samuel W. Adams, Midshipman John L. Cummings, Lieutenant Dulaney Forrest, Midshipman John B. Montgomery, Midshipman Robert S. Tatem, Sailing Master Nelson Webster, and Lieutenant John J. Yarnall, in Jarvis, *A Biographical Notice Of Com. Jesse D. Elliott,* 433-444; accounts of the Battle of Lake Erie by Breese, Brownell, Champlin, Stevens, Taylor, and Turner, Perry Papers, WLCL; diary of Samuel Hambleton, entry of 12 October 1813; Barclay court-martial proceedings, in *Document Transcriptions of the War of 1812*, Volume IV, 4. During the Barclay court-martial the question was asked if the principal injury to the *Queen Charlotte* was received from the *Niagara*, whereupon the reply given was: "No, from the *Caledonia* who laid on our Beam with two long twenty-four pounders on Pivets [sic] also out of Carronade Shot distance."

[80] Dodge, *Battle of Lake Erie*, 15-17; Roosevelt, *Naval War of 1812*, 260-261; Altoff, "A Bulldog of a Naval Gun," 14-17. Of the five American vessels then engaged, the *Lawrence* and *Niagara* each could throw 300 pounds per broadside, although as indicated, the *Niagara* had shifted her larboard 12-pounder bow chaser to the starboard side. The *Scorpion* carried one 32-pounder long gun and either a 32- or a 24-pounder carronade, both on pivots; it is not certain if the *Scorpion* was within carronade range. The *Ariel* fired four 12-pounder long guns, possibly all on pivots, but there is some question as to whether the small pilot vessel had sufficient deck space to mount four tandem 12-pounders; two of the *Ariel*'s guns may have been in broadside, configured with pivots situated on bow and stern with broadside guns fixed amidships. As mentioned, the *Caledonia* mounted two 24-pounder long guns and one 32-pounder carronade, all on pivots. The four smaller gunboats were still astern and hence not yet engaged.

[81] Parsons, *Battle of Lake Erie, A discourse*, 12; Dutton, *Oliver Hazard Perry*, 153.

[82] Pension application file of William Johnson, War of 1812 Pension Application Files, NARA.

[83] Pension application file of David Christie, op. cit.

[84] Pension application file of John Garwood, op. cit.

[85] Bunnell, *Travels and Adventures*, 117.

[86] Parsons, "A Diary Kept During The Expedition To Lake Erie," entry of 12 September 1813.

[87] Pension application file of George Cornell, War of 1812 Pension Application Files, NARA.

[88] Pension application files of William Thompson, John Burdeen, Andrew Mattison, George Varnum, Charles Van Dyke, and Jeremiah Easterbrook, op. cit.

[89] Pension application file of Samuel Hambleton, op. cit.; Hambleton diary, entry of 12 October 1813; Usher Parsons, "Brief Sketches of the Officers Who Were In The Battle Of Lake Erie" in New England Historical and Genealogical Register, Volume 19, #193, 1865, 20.

[90] Ibid.

[91] Parsons, "Brief Sketches of the Officers Who Were In The Battle," 23.

[92] Ibid.; Parsons, "Surgical Account of the Naval engagement on Lake Erie on the 10th September 1813," in New England Journal of Medicine and Surgery, Volume 7, # 4, October 1818, 314.

[93] Parsons, *Battle of Lake Erie, A Discourse*, 13.

[94] Op. cit., 8-12.

[95] Ibid.

[96] Pension application file of William Henry Hight, War of 1812 Pension Application Files, NARA.

[97] Parsons, "Brief Sketches of the Officers Who Were In The Battle," 27.

[98] "List of Killed and Wounded," in *American State Papers*; John Blair Linn, *History of Centre And Clinton Counties, Pennsylvania* (Philadelphia: J.B.

Lippincott & Co., 1883), 51.

[99] Pension application file of William Sloss, War of 1812 Pension Application Files, NARA.

[100] Pension application file of John Lucas, op. cit.

[101] Pension application file of William Smith, op. cit.

[102] Lossing, *Pictorial Field-Book of the War of 1812*, 538.

[103] Pension application file of Isaac Peckham, War of 1812 Pension Application Files, NARA.

[104] "List of Killed and Wounded," in *American State Papers*; Yarnall testimony at the Elliott Court of Inquiry, in Jarvis, *A Biographical Notice Of Com. Jesse D. Elliott*, 436. Yarnall testified that the *Lawrence* had 103 men fit for duty.

[105] Pension application file of Hosea Sergeant, War of 1812 Pension Application files, NARA. Sergeant had been stationed at the aftmost carronade on the starboard side, and evidence suggests that this was probably the final gun to be knocked out of action.

[106] Taylor to Alexander Slidell Mackenzie, 16 January 1841, Taylor Papers, NHS.

[107] Lossing, *Pictorial Field-Book of the War of 1812*, 527f.

[108] Hambleton diary, entry of 12 October 1813.

[109] Ibid.

[110] Major John F. Richardson, K.S.F, *The War of 1812* (Toronto: The Musson Book Co. Limited, 1902), 194; Barclay court-martial proceedings, in *Document Transcriptions of the War of 1812*, Volume IV, 4.

[111] Barclay to Yeo, 12 September 1813, in *Document Transcriptions of the War of 1812*, Volume IV, 43. Barclay related that, "...every Officer commanding Vessels and their seconds was [sic] either Killed or Wounded..." However, Lieutenant John F. Breman, commander of the *Little Belt*, does not appear on the British casualty list, which records no casualties on the smallest British vessel.

[112] Inglis to Barclay, 10 September 1813, *in Document Transcriptions of the War of 1812*, Volume IV, 38-39. Based on the positioning of the vessels, when the *Niagara* was approaching to rake the *Detroit*, Inglis would have been required to swing the British flagship around almost 270° in order to bring the starboard guns to bear. It has been considered that Inglis was simply attempting to wear around enough to bring the remaining larboard guns to bear, but in his letter to Barclay, Inglis states that while "Attempting to Wear to get our Starboard broadside to bear upon [the *Niagara*], a number of the Guns of the Larboard broadside being at this time disabled, [the *Detroit*] fell on board the *Queen Charlotte*...."

[113] This theory has been advanced by Walter Rybka, currently the captain of the U.S. Brig *Niagara*, home-ported in Erie, Pennsylvania. Captain Rybka has studied data pertaining to the maneuverings of the opposing squadrons in great detail. His knowledge and skills make him a leading authority on this complex aspect of the engagement.

[114] Inglis to Barclay, 10 September 1813, *in Document Transcriptions of the War of 1812*, Volume IV, 38-39.

[115] Perry to Jones, 13 September 1813, in Dudley (ed.), *The Naval War of 1812*, Volume II, 557-559.

[116] Pension application file of John Reems, War of 1812 Pension Application Files, NARA.

[117] Pension application files of Sanford A. Mason and George McManomy, op. cit.

[118] Pension application files of John Bellamy and James Lansford, op. cit.

[119] Pension application file of Roswell Hall, op. cit.

[120] Pension application file of Mrs. Elizabeth Trapnell, op. cit.; 1 March 1814 muster roll of Captain Joseph Belt, Muster Rolls of Regular Army Organizations, War of 1812, NARA. Belt's muster roll documents that Schofield died at Bass Island on 20 September 1813.

[121] Pension application file of William B. Brady, op. cit.

[122] William T. Taliaferro to Alfred Thomas Goodman, 21 September 1861, Alfred Thomas Goodman papers, Western Reserve Historical Society, Cleveland, Ohio.

[123] Pension application file of Godfrey Bowman, War of 1812 Pension Application Files, NARA.

[124] Pension application file of Harvey C. Harrington, op. cit.

[125] Pension application file of Patrick FitzPatrick, op. cit.

[126] Thomas Holdup Stevens to Richard M. Johnson, 21 March 1828, in the pension application file of Patrick Fitzpatrick, op. cit.

[127] Inglis to Barclay, 10 September 1813, *in Document Transcriptions of the War of 1812*, Volume IV, 38-39.

[128] Ibid.

[129] Facsimile of Perry's dispatch reproduced in Lossing, *Pictorial Field-Book of the War of 1812*, 530. Perry's message was inaccurate. The British squadron was actually composed of two ships, one brig, two schooners, and one sloop.

[130] Perry to Jones, 10 September 1813, Records of the Department of the Navy, Captains' Letters, NARA.

[131] "List of Killed and Wounded," in *American State Papers*; "Samuel Hambleton's account of the Distribution of prize money on Lake Erie," in op. cit.; Muster Rolls of Regular Army Organizations, War of 1812, NARA; Usher Parsons diary. Those who died from wounds were Thomas Claxton, Francis Cummings, William Davis, Edward Martin, John Newen, George Schofield, Joshua Trapnell, and Henry Vanpool.

[132] "List of Killed and Wounded," in American State Papers; War of 1812 Pension Application Files, NARA. The additional casualties were John Bellamy, William B. Brady, Ebenezer Cunningham, Patrick Fitzpatrick, Samuel Garwood, Josiah Goodrich, James Gray, Harvey C. Harrington, William Henry Hight, Isaac Peckham, Thomas Simms, William Smith, and Asel Wilkinson. Virtually all

written accounts, including the recapitulation on the casualty list itself, specify that the second American brig suffered two men killed and 25 wounded, but the casualty list, as reproduced in the *American State Papers*, only enumerates the names of 23 wounded on the *Niagara*.

[133] Altoff, *Deep Water Sailors - Shallow Water Soldiers*, 37-41. These pages provide an analysis of the variables concerning the number of Americans on board the U.S. Lake Erie squadron.

[134] Hambleton to Perry, 26 May 1814, Perry papers, WLCL.

[135] "List of Killed and Wounded," in *American State Papers*.

[136] "A List of Killed and Wounded in His Majestys [sic] Ships and Vessels under mentioned Action with an American Squadron on Lake Erie Upper Canada 10th. Septr. 1813," in *Document Transcriptions of the War of 1812*, Volume IV, 39-42.

[137] Douglas Hendry, Charles C. Morrisey and David Curtis Skaggs, "British Personnel at the Battle of Lake Erie," in *Inland Seas*, Volume 54, Winter 1998, Number 4, 298-314.

[138] Severance (ed.), "The Dobbins Papers," 350. Prisoner lists reveal that a large number of captured British crewmen were on board the *Lawrence* when the burial ceremony occurred.

[139] The six officers were: Lieutenant Robert Finnis, Royal Navy, commanding officer, *Queen Charlotte*; Lieutenant John Garland, Royal Navy, first lieutenant, *Detroit*; Lieutenant James Garden, Royal Newfoundland Regiment, acting Marine officer, *Queen Charlotte*; Lieutenant John Brooks, U.S. Marine Corps, *Lawrence*; Midshipman Henry Laub, U.S. Navy, *Lawrence*; Midshipman John Clark, U.S. Navy, *Scorpion*.

[140] Perry to Jones, 20 September 1813, 24 September 1813, (?) September 1813, Captains Letters, NARA.

[141] Quoted in Pierre Burton, *Flames Across The Border: The Canadian-American Tragedy, 1813-1814* (Boston: Little, Brown and Company, 1981), 183.

[142] Perry to Jones, 7 October 1813, Captains Letters, NARA.

[143] Isaac Shelby to William Henry Harrison, 21 April 1816, Perry Papers, WLCL.

[144] John Sugden, *Tecumseh's Last Stand* (Norman: University of Oklahoma Press, 1985), 58.

[145] Sources referenced to recount the Battle of the Thames River include: Sandy Antal, *A Wampum Denied, Procter's War of 1812* (Carleton University Press, 1997); Freeman Cleaves, *Old Tippecanoe, William Henry Harrison and His Time* (New York: Charles Scribner's Sons, 1939); Benson J. Lossing, *The Pictorial Field-Book of the War of 1812* (New York: Harper & Brothers, Publishers, 1868); Robert B. McAfee, *History of the Late War in the Western Country* (Bowling Green, Ohio: Historical Publications Company, 1919) Centenary Edition; Major John Richardson, K.S.F., *The War of 1812* (Toronto: The Musson Book Co. Limited, 1902); John Sugden, *Tecumseh's Last Stand* (Norman: University of Oklahoma Press, 1985); Colonel Bennett H. Young, *The Battle of the Thames with*

a List of the Officers and Privates Who Won the Battle (Louisville: John P. Morton and Company, 1903).

[146] Shadrach Byfield, "A Common Soldier's Account," in John Gellner (ed.) *Recollections of the War of 1812: three eyewitnesses' accounts originally published between 1828 and 1854* (Toronto: Baxter Publishing Co., 1964), 26.

[147] Excerpt from the Barclay court-martial proceedings, reproduced in Robert Buckie, "'His Majesty's Flag Has Not Been Tarnished:' The Role of Robert Heriot Barclay," in The Journal of Erie Studies, Fall 1988, Volume 17, Number 2, 98-99.

[148] Barclay to Yeo, 12 September 1813, in Ibid.

[149] Perry to Jones, 25 October 1813, Captains Letters, NARA.

[150] Jarvis, *A Biographical Notice of Com. Jesse D. Elliott*, 226.